MW01200417

Dedication

*This book is dedicated to the countless number
of teachers who took on the tremendous
responsibility of educating and inspiring the students
of Newaygo County. Their dedication to motivating
and challenging the minds of their pupils helped to
shape and define many future careers and lives.*

Acknowledgements

*We wish to thank all the former students who
contributed their childhood memories and class
photos for this project. Without their generous
contribution and support, this project would not
have been possible.*

Table of Contents

Table of Contents

Don't Lose Your Pluck

When things are running crosswise,
　And the engine's out of gear,
When the road is rough and rocky,
　And the sky is far from clear,
When you're plainly up against it and
　You're surely out of luck,
That's the time to use your courage
　And to show your stock of pluck.

'Most any one can travel on a road
　That's smooth and clear,
And any one can get there if he
　Only has to steer;
But when the motor's balky and
　You're running in the muck,
If you're ever going to get there you
　Must call upon your pluck.

Inspirational Poster No. 32

School Poster Co., 1863-5-7 Horton Ave., Grand Rapids, Mich.

Introduction

Michigan's education history can be traced back to the laws created by the colonists in the early 1600's. Colonial education concentrated on reading, writing and religion (and later Latin). As early as 1647 towns with 50 families or more were required by law to start an elementary school. These laws laid the framework for Michigan's education system.

The area that is now Michigan was originally part of the Northwest Territory which was established after the English won the French and Indian War. Congress passed the Northwest Ordinance in 1787 which provided the guidelines for new territories to follow in order to be admitted as a state. The Ordinance of 1787 stated "Religion, morality and knowledge being necessary to good government and the happiness of mankind, schools and the means of education shall forever be encouraged." A provision of the ordinance set aside the 16th section of land in every township for the support of public schools.

Congress established the District School System in the early 1800's which provided for the collection of taxes to fund school operations.

The Michigan Territory was created out of the Northwest Territory in 1805 and by 1823 townships were established. The Statute of 1827 was passed requiring any township with at least 50 families to support a school by public taxation. The statute could be waived if two-thirds of the voters in the township rejected it.

From the Statute of 1827, the township unit school system was developed which allowed local school districts to be established within a township. It also established regulations for school organization. Three directors and a township board of five members acted as inspectors of the schools with the responsibility of overseeing the school districts and giving teacher examinations.

After Michigan became a state in 1837, the Legislature established the school district as a subdivision of the township and each school district was to be governed by a three-member board (director, moderator, and treasurer). Later, a county Commissioner of Schools was elected to oversee all the school districts within a county. The original primary school law enacted in 1837 only required rural schools to teach reading, writing and arithmetic. Other subjects were recommended by the State Superintendent, but each township's school officials created their own school curriculum.

Since the early schools did not have a graded system, students were taught together regardless of age or grade level. After 1850, compulsory school attendance laws were passed requiring students to attend school until they completed a certain grade or reached a certain age. The major problem with this system was that each school had students graduating with vastly different course studies. The students who continued their education at a high school often found themselves lacking in certain subjects.

The County Board of School Examiners was created in 1881 to help develop a uniform system of grading, classification and course of study. A teacher from Newaygo County is credited with developing the first completely graded rural school in the state of Michigan. William E. Gould, who taught for several years at Brookside School in Sheridan Township, started developing the graded classification at Brookside in 1883 and completed the process in 1886. But getting all the school districts to accept a uniform graded system wasn't easy. Officials at both the county and township levels resisted the measure for several years before it was finally implemented in the late 1890's.

The Rural Agricultural School Act was passed in 1917 which allowed three or more adjoining school districts to combine with just one governing board for all the schools rather than a board for each school. It also allowed for both state aid for operations and funds for transporting students to area high schools.

Education was important to the early settlers of Newaygo County. Initially they held "school" in a home or back room of a business until there were enough families in the township or city to officially establish a school district. As the student populations fluctuated, so did the number and boundaries of school districts. Fractional districts were formed when a school district's boundaries entered into another township other than where the school was located. This was necessary because township tax funds were used to support the schools and each township needed to pay its portion according to what fraction of population was located in each school district.

The one-room country school era eventually came to an end as increased populations and better developed city governments changed the educational school system. The majority of Newaygo County's country schools consolidated into the city schools in 1965.

The history of Newaygo County's one-room schools has been scattered over the last 160 years. Much of the history of those very early schools has been lost to time. Almost 50 years has passed since the last classes were held in the one-room country schools. This book is an attempt to record the history and memories of those bygone school years.

✳ ✳ ✳ ✳ ✳ ✳

Special Note

The Newaygo County Society of History and Genealogy staff have made every attempt to give accurate information about the schools in this book. Many records of the early schools have been lost to time and memories may not be what they once were. Please accept our apologies for any errors found in the following pages. We welcome corrections and identifications of unknown students in the photos. We are also including pictures which have not been identified and would appreciate any help our readers can give us to put names to these photos. Contact the Society by email at newaygocohistory@yahoo.com by mail at NCSHG, PO Box 68, White Cloud, MI 49349, or stop by the NCSHG office at 1099 E. Wilcox (next to the post office) in White Cloud.

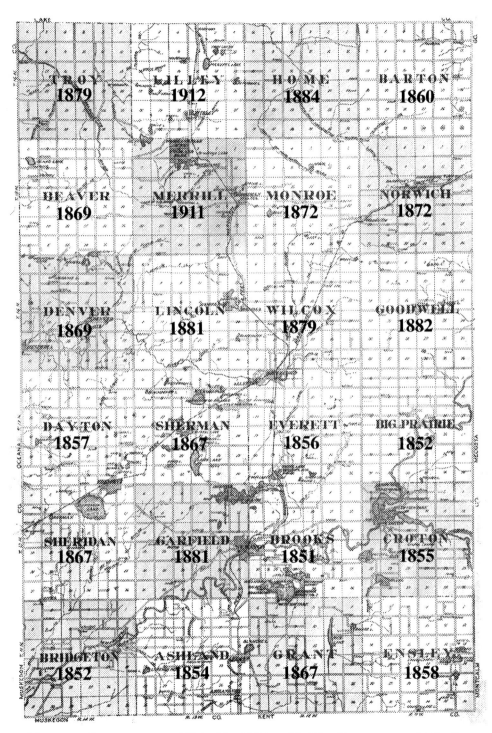

Newaygo County was established in 1851 and is 24 miles across and 36 miles long. It is divided into 24 townships which are all six by six square miles. This 1922 map shows the location and establishment date for each township.

One Room Schools: Architecture
A presentation of the Clark Historical Library

Although simple buildings, one-room school houses developed a distinctive architectural appearance. Almost invariably the first "school house" in a rural district consisted of a log cabin. The log cabin schools, while minimally functional, really were not very well adapted to the needs of the students or teachers. As time passed new school buildings became similar to houses in their construction. The gabled vestibules and bell towers of frame schools also showed the influences of church architecture. To help local school districts construct adequate buildings, the state was issuing "standard" plans for rural schools by the 1890's.

In 1914 the Michigan Department of Public Instruction asked that standard rural schools conform to various specifications. The buildings should rest on at least one-half acre of land, with trees and shrubs "tastefully arranged" about the building. Two "widely separated" outhouses or "indoor sanitary closets" should be provided for the student's use. The building should have a room heater and ventilator or basement furnace. The floors should be of hardwood and lighting should be so arranged so that neither the teachers nor the students should have to face into windows while doing their work. The state also called for "good blackboards, some suitable for small children," and "attractive interior decorations".

In the 1930's the federal government used Work Projects Administration (WPA) funds to make improvements in all "standard" one-room schools. These improvements included the installation of a furnace to replace room heaters, inside chemical toilets to replace those outhouses that remained, and windows on at least one wall of the building, usually situated so that the light would come in over the students left shoulders.

County School Notes, September 19, 1901 - Newaygo Republican

"Called to the attention of the school boards and teachers of the county to the law requiring the display of the United States flag every day during school hours. This law is mandatory and bears a fine for neglect."

Memories of the One Room School

By Howard Douglas

Here is a little of this and that regarding the rural schools 55 years and more ago. This was an era that would seem hard to present-day elementary children and teachers. In 1921, when I started teaching, there were approximately 125 rural schools in Newaygo County, most of them the one-room variety. All eight grades were taught and sometimes "Beginners" as well. The school year was usually of 8 to 9 months duration. The school day was 9:00 to noon and 1:00 to 4:00 with recesses of 15 minutes forenoons and afternoons with longer periods for lower grades. Children walked to school, some for as far as two and a half miles. If weather was too inclement they might ride. No plowed roads either, unless a big brother or father might break trail through the deeper drifts. Lunches, of course, were cold, and for some pitifully meager. Clothing for some was inadequate, especially footwear. No derogatory remarks were made directly to the child. Buildings were cold on a frosty morning as the fire was generally allowed to go out. Toilets were of the outside variety and required paths to be shoveled when snow got too deep.

Each school district was officered by a Director, Moderator, and Treasurer. An Annual Meeting was held each July. At this meeting one officer was elected, millage was levied, school term set, and such other business as was pertinent. The hiring of the teacher was vested in the School Board. The head of all elementary schools in the county was the County School Commissioner. Bonded indebtedness was seldom, if ever, carried.

The School Commissioner at this time was Miss Carrie L. Carter. Miss Carter was the most remarkable and unforgettable woman I have ever known. She was of unbounded energy, a remarkable memory, much talent, and great enthusiasm which she could impart to her teachers and children alike. She served on the State Library Board and was an ardent Granger. She carried on all these activities with very little office help. She visited each school at least once a year, driving her own car over uncertain roads and sometimes in quite inclement weather. How we all enjoyed her visits. She always gave response by calling each by name and giving them much attention, inquiring about their family pets, activities, etc. Her memory was astounding. If she happened to be at the school during the lunch hour she would talk familiarly with them as she ate her lunch…the children giving her some goodies which they had in their lunch pails. She always accepted them with good grace. How they loved her and confided in her. She would observe the teacher, working on some office work as she did so, her eagle eye not seeming to miss a move. She always taught a class, generally a language group, which she animated highly and used up enough time for three ordinary classes. After an hour or so she would depart leaving a sheet of criticism on the desk. Never an oral word. To many of us who were young and experienced these visits were most useful and invigorating.

Wages in those small schools were small, accommodations were limited, work was strenuous, certification was not great, but dedication was great as was the respect for the "teacher" in the community as well as in the school room. A Christmas program was a must and some school boards inserted a clause in the contract calling for a Thanksgiving dinner.

We taught from a syllabus which was the course of study put out by the State Board of Education and to be followed closely. It provided a wealth of materials, guides, and goals for each grade in detail. The goal for eighth graders was a final examination at the end of the year. These tests were made up at the state level and would be given at some central point on a set date. They lasted two days. These tests were "steep" and really separated the men from the boys.

For many it was back to the drawing board for another try next year. A passing of this test was necessary for entrance to high school. Penmanship was stressed to a point where we were told when to teach it. This time was just prior to the first recess when the child's muscles were most relaxed. Reading in the seventh grade was also stressed and a state exam held in the spring.

Organizing classes to fit the day was quite a problem. We did not teach science as such but we did teach agriculture and orthography. We did much singing, using Henry Pattengill's "Pat's Pick". What we lacked in technique we made up in enthusiasm and gusto. Everyone sang with no thoughts of jibes for sour notes or off keys. Playtime was important. It was seldom organized but fit the season and moods. The teacher often participated with old and young playing the same games. The games we played were so different than children play today, many of them unheard of today. What an atmosphere to grow up in and what a means for the teacher to have to get to understand their children. Punishment was meted out with surprising fairness probably due to the closeness of teacher and student.

There were certain taboo subjects, such as politics - local and outside, to be shunned and not entered into. Gossip was not to leave the classroom and family "bits" were not to be strewn about however ludicrous they might be. Poor wearing apparel, lunches, etc. were never discussed.

With all its hard work and inconveniences, teaching was only a part of the job. Fires must be built, water pumped, floors swept, snow shoveled, cleaning, etc. The work was rewarding and mingling with young minds and helping them develop socially as well as academically was always a pleasure.

But this era would not last long. Another decade would find integration setting in. Schools would be consolidated into larger groups and only a memory of yesteryear remains, but from these little school units came high school valedictorians, college graduates, and successful business people. The lessons they learned here were not all academic by any means and after all isn't that an important part of a successful program.

Newaygo County Normal

A normal school was a school created to train high school graduates to be teachers. Its purpose was to establish teaching standards or norms, hence its name. American normal schools were intended to improve the quality of the burgeoning common school system by producing more qualified teachers.

Prior to the formation of the normal school, strict memorization was the primary teaching method used in the United States. The normal schools encouraged a process of critical thinking and guidance as preferable teaching methods. Another normal school in Ridgewater, Massachusetts, graduated class of 26 who went on to lead normal schools in other states, including Illinois and Michigan. The first normal school west of the Appalachian Mountains in the United States was the Michigan State Normal School, now Eastern Michigan University. It was created by legislative action in 1848 and opened in Ypsilanti, Michigan in 1853.

As the concept of the normal school spread to other states, the idea of teaching education expanded to incorporate model classrooms and a learning laboratory environment. Typically, the normal school program was two years in length. Many normal schools, promoting the art and science of teaching, were established in the U.S. during 1870-90. To supplement the normal schools, county-level teacher institutes were also held.

By the 1920s, the term "normal school" lost ground to the preferable term "teachers' college." At this time, most such educational institutions were also restructured into four year programs that granted degrees in teacher education. In the United States, the function of normal schools has been taken up by undergraduate and graduate schools of education; the schools themselves were upgraded to universities focused on meeting the needs of the region in which they were located.

The county normal school in Newaygo County was established in Fremont and was a small brick building that had been a restroom for Fremont Public Schools. The building was remodeled and used for the County Normal Training School. Applicants received a completion certificate which enabled them to teach children ages five to eighteen. The Normal School was discontinued in 1920 for lack of room. The building was torn down when the last unit of the school building was constructed in 1926. Many of the applicants after 1920 attended Western State Normal College (WSNC). It's name later changed to Western State Teacher's College (WSTC) and eventually the name was changed to what it is known as today, Western Michigan University.

*First Graduating
Class of 1906*

*June 13, 1906
- The first gradu-
ating class of the
Newaygo County
Normal posed
for their picture:
standing (left to
right),   Bessie
Kuypers, Nora
E. Mast, Harriet
Sage, Katherine*

*Stroven, May Joslin; seated, middle row, Helen Stuart, Adeline Hoose, Carrie L.
Carter (instructor), Addie Coil, Vera Tyler; front row, Clara Taylor, Minnie Seymour,
Fausta Starn*

*50 Year
Reunion June
1956*

*A reunion in
White Cloud
brought togeth-
er all but three
of the graduat-
ing class. Miss
Carter had
passed away
some years*

*earlier. Standing, left to right, Miss Nora E. Mast of White Cloud, Mrs. May Joslin
Brower of Newaygo, Mrs. Harriet Sage Vickstrom of Fremont, Mrs. Adeline Hoose
Robertson of E. Lansing, Mrs. Vera Tyler Teskey of St. Clair Shores; seated, Mrs.
Minnie Seymour Hoyt of Fremont, Mrs. Fausta Starn O'Neil of Fremont, Miss Kath-
erine Stroven of Fremont, Miss Bessie Kuypers of Muskegon Heights.*

Teacher's Test
The following test was offered in April of 1882 to anyone who desired to be certified to teach the third grade. Are you qualified to teach this school?

GRAMMAR
1. What is the chief object of studying grammar?
2. What is a compound sentence?
3. Define I, it, she
4. Compare thin, bottomless, good, matured, first, lovely.
5. Give the principal part of lay, fly, do, see, lie, (to recline).
6. Write synopsis of "go" in the indicative and the potential mood, first person singular, active voice.
7. Write the plurals of: deer, oasis, cherry, chimney, sister-in-law, phenomenon, this. Analyze the following sentences:
8. The man who escapes censure, is fortunate.
9. Henry, go home, immediately.
10. Correct the following sentences and give reasons for the changes:
    a. Which is the largest number, the minuend or the subtrahend?
    b. He told John and I to speak gentler to the children.
    c. Detroit has the greatest population of any other city in Michigan.
    d. He could not deny but what he borrowed the money.
    e. Neither James nor John have had three perfect lessons this week.

U.S. HISTORY
1. In what year was the battle of Buena Vista fought, and who were the commanders on each side?
2. Name a State, now in the Union, which was once recognized by United States as an independent Republic, and tell how long it remained such a Republic.
3. What was the purpose and object of the Fugitive Slave Law?
4. Name the statesman who said, "if that be treason make the most of it", and tell under what circumstances he made the remark.
5. When and where did the First Continental Congress meet and what did it do?
6. What is meant by the Alabama claims and the Geneva award?
7. When and where was the first gun fired in the late rebellion, and tell who were the commanders on each side.
8. Give the name of the statesman who championed the right of petition in the halls of Congress and carried on a single-handed contest for eleven days before he won the victory.
9. Were any duels ever fought between American statesmen, and if so give names, dates, and particulars.
10. Name an American Statesman who was assaulted in Congress by a Southern member with a cane, and tell the cause of the assault and the effect of it upon the person assaulted.

ARITHMETIC

1. Find the greatest common measure and the least common multiple of 32, 42, and 64.
2. How is the value of a fraction changed by increasing its denominator? Give the reason.
3. Find the value of 2-3x3-5 divided by 7/8 expressed decimally.
4. Divide seven ten thousandths by fourteen thousand. Explain the process giving the reason for pointing off.
5. There are 394 sq. feet 2'9" in the floor of a hall that is 10 feet 7" wide; what is its length?
6. What is the better investment, to buy sugar at 7 ½ cents a pound, on a 4 months time, or at 8 cents a pound on 6 months, money being worth 6 per cent?
7. Find the square root of 42846 and tell how you would explain the process to the class?
8. Divide 7/9 by 4.5 and tell how you would explain the process to the class?
9. Three persons buy a piece of land for $4,569 paying in the following proportions viz: the sum of the first and second, the sum of the first and third, and the sum of the second and third, are to each other as 1-2 3-5 and 7-10; how much did each pay and what part did each own?
10. A, B, and C can do a piece of work worth $30 in 4 days; A can do it in 10 days, B in 12 days, A works 3 days, B 2 days and C 1 day. B and C finish the work. What will be each one's share of the money, provided each is paid according to the time it takes him to do the work?

CIVIL GOVERNMENT

1. Name the presiding officers of the two houses of the State Legislature, and tell how they are chosen?
2. How many jury men are required to try criminal cases in justice courts and how are they chosen?
3. Of how many judges is the U.S. Supreme Court composed, and how are they chosen and for how long?
4. Who is the chief Justice of the United States?
5. What is meant by free trade and protection, and which one of the two has been the prevailing policy of the United States government?
6. What is a sumptuary law? Give an example of one.
7. What is an expost facto law, as used in the Constitution of the United States?
8. What is a writ of Habeas Corpus, and under what circumstances does the U.S. Constitution permit it to be suspended?
9. How often does the Legislature of Michigan meet?
10. What is a reciprocity treaty?

THEORY AND ART OF TEACHING

1. At what age, or at what stage of their progress should children begin the study of grammar?
2. How would you teach a class of beginners in this study? How, an advanced class?
3. Why is it important that a teacher should have a knowledge of physiology and hygiene?
4. Would you permit pupils to remain in the school-room during recess?
5. Would you ever join them in their games?
6. What is the object of a recitation?
7. How much time each day or week would you give to teaching morals?
8. How would you induce parents and district officers to visit your school?
9. Why is it important that you attend the bi-monthly meeting of the Teacher's Association?
10. Why do you wish to be a teacher, give four reasons.

GEOGRAPHY

1. In what direction is Cincinnati from San Francisco?
2. Where is the Caspian Sea, and name the chief river that flows into it?
3. How many mouths had the Danube River, and into what do they flow?
4. What is Majorca Island, and to what group does it belong?
5. Name the largest state in the United States.
6. Name three of the largest rivers in Michigan.
7. About what proportion of the state of Georgia is sea coast?
8. What direction would you take in going on a straight line from Ireland to Austria and from Ireland to New Foundland.
9. Name the capital city of Persia.
10. What is Mount Sinai?

ORTHOGRAPHY

1-5. 1 Parallels 2 Usually 3 Tour 4 Tassel 5 Turbine 6 Raspberry 7 Pristine 8 Plateau 9 Orchestra 10 Nausea 11 Encove 12 Exemplary 13 Deficit 14 Wednesday 15 Prairie 16 Apostasy 17 Artesian 18 Ascension 19 Bicycle 20 Bivouac 21 Bowieknife 22 Dyspepsia 23 Fogginess 24 Glycerine 25 Gauge
6. What is a diphthong?
7. How many diphthongal sounds?
8. Explain the difference between separable and insuperable diphthongs?
9. What is a diagraph?
10. What is essential to every syllable?

PENMANSHIP

1. Describe the position you prefer for writing at a desk.
2. Would you drill your pupils in any other?
3. Show by diagram the principles of the small letters.
4. What is the length in spaces of t, p, f, g?
5. Show by diagram the principles of the capital letters.
6. How would you teach a penmanship class?

MY WORK

Let me but do my work from day to day,
  In field or forest, at the desk or loom,
  In roaring market place or tranquil room;
Let me but find it in my heart to say,
When vagrant wishes beckon me astray—
  "This is my work; my blessing, not my
  doom.
  Of all who live I am the one by whom
This work can best be done in the right way."

Then shall I find it not too great nor small,
  To suit my spirit and to prove my powers;
  Then shall I cheerful greet the laboring
  hours.
And cheerful turn, when the long shadows fall,
  At eventide to play and love and rest,
  Because I know for me my work is best.

                                        —HENRY VAN DYKE

Inspirational Poster No. 27

School Poster Co., 1803-5-7 Horton Ave., Grand Rapids, Mich.

County Examination

By Tom LaBelle "LaBelle at Large"

County Examinations were the climax of rural education in Michigan in the 1920s and 1930s. They were held the first week of May. It took a month or so to find out if you passed or flunked.

On examination day, the 12 and 13-year-olds arrived in their Sunday clothes, each clutching his own bottle of ink, a steel point pen, a roll of white, lined "legal cap" paper and his lunch.

They assembled in a large room. The county school commissioner addressed them briefly. Then, teacher-monitors deployed themselves and the examination sheets were distributed. It began.

"What is meant by the Articles of Confederation."

"Write a time, interest-bearing, negotiable, promissory note."

"Tell briefly the early history of Pennsylvania."

"Draw a diagram showing a farm described as the S ½ of the NE ¼ of the section, and locate a drain that begins 20 rods south of the northeast corner of the farm and extends west to the west line, thence north on the west line to the north line. How many rods long is this drain?"

The questions went on, page after page. After lunch there were tests of spelling, penmanship and poetry recitation, including interpretation and definition.

Dr. Austin Lamberts, former Grand Rapids neurosurgeon and now a research marine biologist, remembers the tests from his Newaygo County school days.

"There was a test for seventh graders and one for eighth graders, and you couldn't be promoted from either grade without passing it. I think if you asked some of the questions of 12 and 13-year-olds today, they'd have trouble."

Teachers and student in Michigan rural schools sweated for months to get ready, he said.

"If you failed by just a few points, you had a chance to take the test again. The pass rate was pretty good, but some people kept taking the test and repeating the grade until they were 16 and could quit school."

Lamberts said he'd been hearing about modern junior high, and even high school, graduates who have been shown to be poor readers. He grew curious about whether the County Examinations in his day (late 1920's) – which, if you couldn't at least read, would be impossible to pass – could have been as tough as he remembered.

He wrote to Leon Deur, retired Newaygo County school superintendent. Deur told him none of the old tests were on file. However, his wife, Fay, another County Examinations veteran, had saved her test questions. She was happy to let Lamberts borrow them.

He needed only one look. If anything, he said, nostalgia had softened the memory.

Lamberts concedes the times were different. Elementary education was laid on powerfully "with the assumption this was all the education a lot of the students would ever get."

The experience was so vivid for Mrs. Henrietta Smalligan of Fremont that on the second Thursday and Friday of May each year, no matter what else she happens to be doing, the memory comes flooding back.

Mrs. Loretta Slowinski of Orleans kept a copy of her test questions for 62 years, including the questions from the part of the test she flunked and had to take a second time.

Others have called or written to share their impressions of the old County Examinations, the ordeal of May which, before the days of consolidation, climaxed all rural school education in Michigan.

What brought the reaction was a recent column about the examinations. The column was inspired by a talk with another veteran of Michigan rural education, Dr. Austin Lamberts, of Grand Rapids.

Dr. Lamberts has a theory that modern seventh and eighth graders, faced with such a test, would either be better readers than they reportedly are or would be condemned to repeat seventh grade indefinitely.

Dr. Lamberts' brother, Mayor Peter Lamberts of Kentwood, also took the County Examinations and later taught in a rural school.

He said the old rural system lacked the prestige of city schools (whose students didn't have to take County Examinations) but they had advantages.

For one thing, he said, it was almost an "open" school. All the grades were thrown together. The lower grade students were exposed to what the upper grades were doing.

"Believe me," Lamberts said, "that was a big help."

Also, in those hard-scrabble times, the quality of rural teachers tended to be high. Excellent teachers-to-be attended County Normal because it was the only teaching education they could afford, and then began their careers in one or two-room rural schools.

Lamberts cited two examples from his own Newaygo County system, Albert Zagers, retired superintendent of Godfrey-Lee schools here and Julia Timmer, retired assistant superintendent at Godwin.

Even if the teachers weren't excellent, the County Examinations backstopped the program. If a teacher didn't get his students up for the County Examinations, his career was in danger of early abortion.

In some areas he might be lucky if the farmer-parents whose kids all flunked didn't want a piece of his scalp.

Mrs. Slowinski sent a Xerox of her 1916 test questions, together with the introduction to the test written by Fred. L. Keeler, then Michigan superintendent of public instruction. The introduction, meant to be reassuring, went like this:

"To the eighth grade pupil: I am glad you are going to write on this examination. I hope you will pass. If you have done your work in your schoolroom, you will find this examination easy. Go at it just like an ordinary day's work in your own schoolroom. Remember that the Conductor, the Commissioner and the State Superintendent are all your friends and are anxious to see you succeed..."

Then bang,

Name four conditions that will injure the eyes; two things that will injure the ear; three things that will cause the teeth to decay.

In what states of the United States are the following the leading products: cotton, coal, petroleum, iron, gold, copper, lumber?

Name the chief exports and imports of Great Britain.

Name the chief exports and imports of the United States.

What had each of the following men to do with Michigan history: Mason, Pierce, Peter White?

And so on the rest of the day, with time out for lunch.

Reorganization Committee Meets

March 25, 1965 local newspaper article

The Newaygo County Intermediate School District Reorganization Study Committee held its first meeting at the courthouse in White Cloud on Tuesday, March 9 for the purpose of organizing the committee and to become oriented to the functions assigned to it by the School District Reorganization Act of 1964.

In keeping with the provisions of the Act, the Intermediate Superintendent of Schools, Leon J. Deur, will act as chairman of the committee. The committee elected Gerald Sherman to serve as vice chairman and Mrs. Laura Ward of Bitely as secretary.

Other members of the committee are: James Bekkering, Fremont; James George, Grant; Lawrence Johnson, Newaygo; Harry Rellinger, Hesperia; Willard McReaken, White Cloud; Wesley Jordan, Croton; Roy Dennis, Pine View; Earl Robinson, Ashland Center; Robert VanderMeulen, Ensley; John Hagman, Big Jackson; Richard Bell, Newaygo; J. Donald Murphy, Fremont; Mrs. Allen Murphy, Wooster; Max Purcell, Garfield Center; Carroll Robinson, Grant and James Ryder, Bitely.

The committee noted that the Act and the State Committee guidelines establish a time table which requires that the local intermediate study committee complete its study within nine months which would mean that the committee recommendation on school district reorganization would be ready for the state committee next January, 1966. Following approval by the state committee the proposed reorganizations are to be presented to the voters within six months. Such elections could possibly be held as early as the fall of 1966.

The committee then reviewed the present school district reorganization in the county. There are 24 non-high school districts and five high school districts. It was noted that most of the non-high school districts send their high school students to one of the five high schools in the county but there are a few high schools bordering the county which provide service within the county also. These include Baldwin, Reed City, Big Rapids, Tri-County (Howard City), and Walkerville.

Announcement was made that two of the districts have already been given approval to hold annexation elections. The Big Jackson district will vote on March 20 to annex to Big Rapids and the Garfield Center district will vote on March 29 to annex to Fremont and Newaygo. Several of the districts are giving study to the possibility of holding an annexation election prior to final action of the Study committee but all such proposed annexations would also have to meet the approval of the Study Committee.

In preparing their recommendations for school district reorganization in Newaygo County, committee members will consider the following:

1. Quality and breadth of future education programs
2. Final abilities of the proposed reorganized school district
3. The effective use of present community centers and service areas
4. Geographical compactness and population density

The committee instructed the representative from each of the high school districts to arrange a meeting in their high school service area to review the reorganization problem in their particular area.

Nora Cook's high school diploma in 1910

Ray Evans' high school diploma in 1908

Big Prairie Township

Big Prairie Township was established in 1852, a year after Newaygo County was formed, making it one of the earliest townships in the county. The original boundaries encompassed the north twenty-four miles of the east half of the county. In 1856, the township was divided in order to add Everett as a new township. From 1856 to 1884, Big Prairie Township's area kept being reduced until it became the area size that is recognized as today. It's official township designation is Township 13 North, Range 11 West.

1900

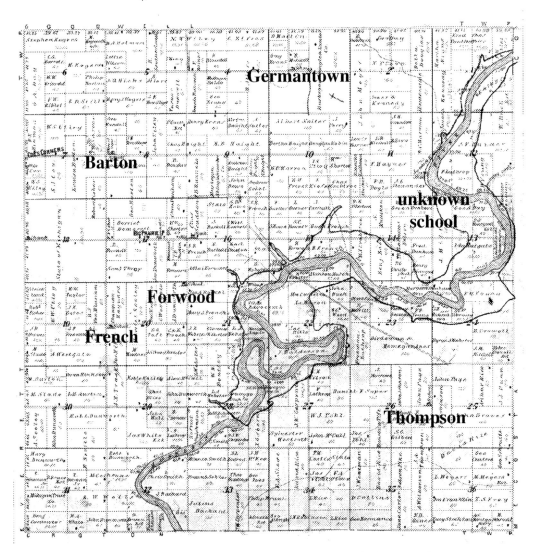

The pencilled in drawing shows how the area changed after Hardy Dam was constructed.

1922

30

MAP OF
BIG PRAIRIE
TOWNSHIP
Scale 2 inches to 1 mile

Township 12 North, Range 11 West of the Michigan Meridian

Germantown

Barton

Big Bend

Forwood

Thompson

Early history of
Big Prairie Township Schools

Once the residents in Big Prairie Township organized a school district in 1850, school was taught in a private home with Relief Bonney as the instructor. Sometime in 1852 the first schoolhouse (School District #1) was built in the center of section 18 with Adelaide Olney as the first teacher. It was constructed of vertically placed boards with a puncheon floor and log seats. A floor made of "puncheons" meant that the floor was made of split logs with the split side turned upwards. This school burned and a new one was built on the west side of the section (18). The school was also used for church services by the Rev. Kelley who came from Newaygo to preach. After the building was abandoned as a school, it was used for funerals due to its location near the cemetery.

In 1884 there were five school districts in Big Prairie Township. For the year ending Sept. 3, 1883, the number of children between the ages of 5 and 20 was 177; number who attended school, 123; number of non-resident pupils, 8; number of days of school taught, 485; number of frame school buildings, 2; number of log school buildings, 3; number of pupils that can be seated, 172; value of school property $1,035; number of male teachers employed 1; number of female teachers employed, 6; wages paid male teachers, $66.65; wages paid female teachers, $61.70.

By the 1930s and possibly earlier, five schools in Big Prairie Township were under one Board: Barton, Germantown, Thompson, Forwood and Big Bend.

This is probably the first school house organized and built in Big Prairie Township by the Ephraim Utley family. Ephraim's son, George, attended school for three winters.

AUCTION SALE

OF

BUILDINGS

BIG PRAIRIE SCHOOL DIST. NO. 1 UNIT WILL SELL AT PUBLIC AUCTION THE FOLLOWING SCHOOL BUILDINGS ON

Saturday, July 27, '46

COMMENCING AT 10 A. M.

THE GERMANTOWN SCHOOLHOUSE, SIZE 36X22 FEET
WOOD SHED 12X18   AND TWO OUTSIDE TOILETS

THE BIG BEND SCHOOL HOUSE, 30X22, AND WOODSHED 14X16

THE BARTON SCHOOL HOUSE, 34X24, AND WOODSHED 14X20

THE FORWOOD SCHOOLHOUSE, 30X20, AND WOOD SHED 12X16

THE THOMPSON SCHOOLHOUSE, 34X22, AND WOOD SHED 14X16

The sale will be held on the school grounds in the following order:

At 10 o'clock a. m. the Germantown School House and wood shed located in SW¼ of NW¼ of Sec. 3, Big Prairie Twp, will be sold, Then the Big Bend School House and wood shed located in NE¼ of NE¼ of Sec. 15, Then the Barton School House and wood shed located in SW¼ of NW¼ of Sec. 8, Then the Forwood School House and shed located in SW¼ of SW¼ of Sec. 16, Then the Thompson School House and wood shed in SE¼ of NE¼ of Sec 26. All these buildings are in Big Prairie Township, Newaygo County.

Big Prairie Ladies Aid will sell lunch at noon at Barton School

TERMS OF SALE: CASH WITHIN TEN DAYS.
A down payment of $200 must be made on the grounds, by cash or certified check

HOPPA AND LAWRENCE, Auct.

In 1946 there was this flyer circulated to advertise the selling of school buildings in Big Prairie: Germantown section 3, Big Bend section 15, Barton section 8, Forwood section 16, Thompson section 26. This flyer also serves as a notice that these schools were all closed by 1946.

Barton School
School District #3

Barton School was located in Section 8 at the corner of 12th Street and Locust. It was also known as Standard School.

Teachers: Jean Ewing, Roy Holmes (1901), Miles Barton, Beth Gilbert, Thelma Garney, Rose Slade (1924), Felma Aishe's first job as a school teacher was at Barton School in 1935. The next year Barton and Germantown Schools consolidated and she taught at Germantown in 1936 for one year.

Students: Jeanette Webster Deur, Jean Barton Puvogel, Carol Barton Wicks, Keith Barton Louise Dunham Linderer, Leo Haight, Helene Southerland Long, Germaine Boucher Carpenter, Hilda Kline.

Barton (Standard) School when it was in use and how it appeared in the 1980's.

Barton School students Spring 1901 – Teacher Roy Holmes from Sparta

Inside of Barton School

Barton (Standard) School students June 1911
Front row: Glen Eash, Kenneth Dayton, Edward Haight, Vera Phillips,
Margaret Terwillegar, William Rauch, Otis Terwillegar, Ward
Sutherland, Wayne Sutherland, Chester Rauch, Bernie Phillip,
Roy Mischler
Back row: Henry Terwillegar, Myrtle Haight, Hilda Terwillegar, Anna Wing,
teacher Myrtle Dunham, Violet Webster, Andrew Goebel, Jessie
Dayton, Alfred Wing

A social gathering at Barton School in 1911

Barton School students
Front row: Ed VanSyckle, Walter Rogers, Maud Rogers, Jennie Barton (standing),
*   teacher Nettie Peters, John Utley (standing), Claudeen VanSyckle, Frank*
*   Cool, Charley Barton*
Middle row: Alex Barton, Murty Rogers, Fern Utley, Fitch Coon, George Cox, Phil
*   Barton, Steve Rogers, Glenn Utley*
Back row: Robert Wells, Lettie Utley, Susie Barton, Della Utley (not a student),
*   Mettie Meyers, Arthur Fisher*

Note: Photo identifications by Fern Utley Dayton when she was 79 years old.

Fern Utley's memories of her first day of school:
    "When I was four years old, my mother was caring for a baby brother, whom my father had given the eminent name of Ossian Thor. After talking with the teacher, a Mrs. Mary Fisher, an old friend and neighbor, she being a kind soul, consented, so with primer in hand I started out in charge of an older sister, Lettie, or Tin as she was then called. In those days girls and boys did not sit together, but on opposite sides of the room. But I had been a playmate and companion of my brother, Glenn, so I insisted on sitting with him on the boy's side. So teacher Mary, to keep peace, gave in. Next was that I was very fond of cats and had several of them. So I hid a kitten under my coat to take to school. About half way to the school, Lettie discovered it, but being anxious to be on time, we went on cat and all. Teacher let me keep it - a second version of "Mary and her Little Lamb." But when I went to get my lunch pail to feed it during class, teacher said that was too much – the cat must go! A small boy named Walter Rogers said he knew where the Utley's lived and was dispatched there with the kitty in spite of my tears.

Frank Cool's snow story:

Frank Cool attended Barton School about 1886 and his teacher was Dell Utley. Some of his classmates were Phil Barton, George, Albert and Datis Cox, and Glen and John Utley. Years ago, he related this story: "I remember the teacher during the winter session gave orders that 'no scholar would be allowed to throw snow into the school building.' However, only a few days had elapsed, when suddenly at the noon hour, some scholars while playing outdoors, began throwing snow into the school building. The teacher went to the door and said 'Stop,' but a very unruly boy spoke up and called her a fool. She then told this boy to 'gather up his books and go home,' which he did. But this boy's parents and the teacher must have patched up their differences, because the next morning the boy was in school."

Barton School students 1909-1910
Front row: Glenn Aishe, unknown, Bill Rauch, Otis Terwillegar, Roy Mishler,
Ward Sutherland, Wayne Sutherland
Back row: Henry Terwillegar?, Mertie Haight, Hilda Terwillegar, ? Wing,
Mertie Dunham, Violet Webster, Jessie Dayton, Alfred Wing.

Big Bend School
School District #7

Big Bend School was originally a log school building which stood where Hardy Pond is now, on the river road three quarters of a mile above Whitney Bridge, or a half mile south and a mile west of what is now Big Bend Park, at the quarterpost between sections 14 and 15.

The school burned down and was rebuilt in 1901. The building was taken down about 1928 and was removed to Stuart Howe's.

Big Bend School

A new frame school was erected in its place and remained there until 1930 when it was moved a quarter mile north up the hill toward Bill Thumser's by John Miller.

John Miller and his wife had sold their farm to Consumers Power Company in 1928 for the purpose of constructing Hardy Dam and flooding the area for what is now referred to as Hardy Pond. The Miller children's father moved Big Bend school house from its original location, taking it across Hardy Dam in its early stages of development, and deposited it in its present location. John F. Miller moved buildings often with his team of horses and using log "rollers." Miller later related that the horses were rather skittish as they moved the school house across the wooden planks on the Hardy Causeway prior to its completion.

The teacher in 1918 was Frank E. Hicks and some of his students were Fern Miller and her sister Frances and brother Neil. Previous Miller siblings that attended the school were Fred, Oliver and Tom.

Big Bend School

Aishe Family

Two sisters that attended Big Bend, Felma and Sadie Aishe, daughters of William and Edith Aishe supplied these memories of the school:

Felma Aishe Gardiner – attended 1921 through 1929, first through 8th grades. The school was named for a big bend in the Muskegon River which partially enclosed the district. She recalls that when Hardy Dam was built, the school was moved to a nearby hilltop to avoid being flooded. She went home for lunches, but some children had peanut butter sandwiches, cookies and apples. They played softball, had foot races, and played Annie I Over the Woodshed and pump, pump, pull away. She recalls having a Christmas program and a last day of school picnic. There were outhouses used. Her teachers were Miss Mabel Allyers, Mrs. Rose Slade, Mrs. Ruth Maile, Miss Hazel Simmons, Mrs. Gladys Toft, and Mr. Jesse Smith. Some of the children who attended school during her years there were LeRoy, Sadie and Lucy Aishe, Lilly Halcomb, Francis Elwell, Dorothy, Louise, Esther, Hazel Dustin, Evelyn, John, Robert, Mary Jane and Betty Moore, Neil and Fern Miller, Ethel, Harry, Harley and Melvin Decker.

Sadie Aishe Westgate – attended Big Bend School 1919 through 1929, age 7½ thru 8th grade. Miss Nellie Taylor was her teacher the first two years there. A male teacher taught one year only as he beat a girl. He beat her with a stick he took out of the wood box and her mother had his certificate taken away. It all came about because the mother was poor and she didn't have money for clothes because her husband had died and she didn't have much means to support them. The girl's shoes were worn and the soles flapped when she walked. Her mother told her to keep her boots on at school. When the teacher told her to take her boots off, she refused saying her mother told her to keep them on. That made him mad so he picked up the piece of wood and beat her with it. Sadie's last teacher, 7th and 8th grade, was Rose Slade. Sadie graduated from Big Bend school at age 17 in 1929 (8th grade). She went home for lunch and recalls playing fox and geese in winter, ring around the rosie, and ball in good weather. There was a Christmas program and a picnic on the last day of school. Some of the children she went to school with over the years were: Neil Miller, Dorothy, Hazel, Louise Dustin, Lillie Holcomb, Evelyn, John, Bob and Helen Moore, Roy, Felma and Lucy Aishe.

Sadie recalls the school layout as boys sitting on the left and the girls sitting on the right. There were closets for boys and girls on either side of the front door and the furnace sat in the right side of the entry door. The teacher and blackboard were opposite the front door.

Other teachers who taught at Big Bend School were Howard Douglas and Hilda Kline.

Other students who attended Big Bend were Ruby Bidelman Wolever and the Troyanowski family.

Fern Miller's Certificate of Promotion to the fifth grade

Big Bend Log School students circa 1899
Teacher - Grace Utley
Front row: Lyle Webster, Thomas Miller, Clyde Crabtree, Alice Crabtree, Beulah
    Webster, Pearl Howe
Middle row: Ray Miller, Fay Priet, Mahlan French, Edmore Westgate, Ina Goebel,
    Loretta Priest, Joseph Howe, Pearl Miller, Glen Webster
Back row: Jasper Priest, Eddie Westgate, Henry O'Conner, Clarence Miller,
    Floyd French, Georgiana O'Conner, Minnie Howe, Minnie Goebel

November 14, 1895 - Newaygo Republican
   "School District 7, Big Prairie Township, report for month ending November 1. 17 pupils enrolled. Roll of honor: Fremont Crabtree, Glen Dunham, Floyd French, Minnie and Ina Goebel. Victor G. Willbur, Teacher.

Forwood School

Forwood School
School District #4

Forwood School originally had a temporary structure built in 1901. A permanent school building was built in 1903 and was located in Section 16 at the corner of 24th and Elm. In 1900 it appears to have been located on an adjacent corner in Section 20.

1901 Newaygo Republican

"The patrons of School District #4, Big Prairie Township, turned out on Monday, April 8 and erected a temporary school house and on the following day, school was commenced."

Teachers: Howard Douglass, Otis Sherer, Rose Slade and Earl Evans.

Students that attended Forwood school: Albert, Alfred, Clifton, Doris, Esther, Gordon, Ralph Webster; Russel, Stanley, Ruth Forwood; Leslie, Mary, David, Margery, Cecil Hole; Louise, Martin, Eunice Perry; George and Elizabeth Arnold, Jewell and Esther Miller; Myrna Spade Stuthard, Jack Hoover and Dorcus Haight, Carolyn Truesdale Siders, Bob Cavender

Forwood School teacher
Otis Sherer

Forwood School students
Doris Webster (Pohl) is the girl front center (X)

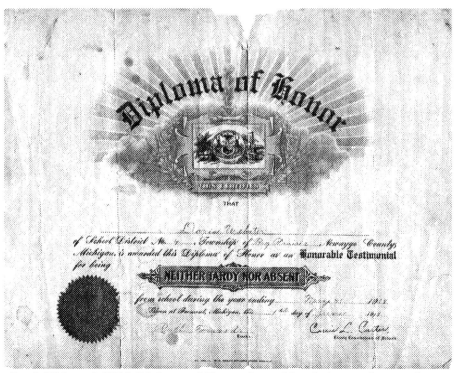

Doris Webster's 1918 Diploma of Honor for neither being tardy nor absent.

District #4 news circa 1910

   "After a Newaygo County Grange meeting held at Big Prairie Township Hall, 30 children from #4 school, with teacher Miles Barton, marched in to violin music, followed by a little girl carrying the U.S. flag. After a salute to the flag, they joined in chorus singing 'Annie Laurie' medleys, rounds and songs, like 'Kentucky Home' and 'Columbia.'"

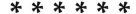

School District #2

   This was a fractional school district which disappeared from the records after 1913. The name of the school is not known. Some of the teachers in District #2, Big Prairie Township: Mrs. Grace Toft Utley (1898), Harry Douglass, Elsie Gifford, (1911), Sibby Gifford (1911), Ida B. Smith; Miss Freida Greene; Miss Terwillegar; Mrs. C. Douglass; Gladys Egolf; Helen Geisa; Nellie Roman (3 month contract starting April 19, 1909); Minnie Buttleman (8 month contract starting Sept. 15, 1907).

French School
AKA Taylor School
School District #1

During the winter of 1855-56 the Taylor School was built on section 20 of Big Prairie Township, about one mile south of Big Prairie Post Office, where Ephraim Utley was postmaster. Inside this schoolhouse, log seats were arranged around the wall. Later, when this building was moved a mile east it became known as French School, this occurred between 1880 and 1900. Miles Barton was a teacher at French School at one point. French School was Newaygo County historian Harry Spooner's first teaching position (1898).

French School students - Miles Barton was the teacher

Special Note:
*Miles Barton was elected probate judge but died
from appendicitis before taking office.*

Germantown School
AKA Libertytown

Germantown School, also known as Libertytown School, was located in Section 3 at the corner of 4th and Cherry Streets.

Nancy Mast Fry taught at Germantown School.

Students that attended Germantown School: Dunham family - Charles, Don, Arlene, Carolyn and Jean (Plowman). Guy Mast (1912)

Germantown/Libertytown School students

Thompson School

Thompson School
School District #10

Thompson School was located in Section 26 and came to life as a log building in 1885 at 36th Street and Beech. In 1905 it was replaced by a cement block building. School was held there until 1946 when it was consolidated with Morley Schools.

The school sat 1/4 mile south of 36th Street on Beech Street. There was a water pump in front of the school, a wood shed directly behind the school, and two outhouses beyond the wood shed.

Upon entering the school, a small foyer held a coat room to the right and a wood box to the left with the bell rope by the box. Walking through another door brought you into the main room with the wood stove on the right. There were 8" block walls, six windows and kerosene lamps on the walls between each window. The floor was wood and at the end of the room was the blackboard and teacher's desk.

Teachers: Ruth Maile, Don Jeffers, Mr. Ewing

Students: Charles Parrott, Lucy Parrott, Hilda Weeks, Jack Schoomaker, Ruth Schoomaker, Kenneth Towne, Edith Towne, Edwin Towne, Arthur Westgate, Donald Westgate, Cecil Decker, June Decker, Donald Howe, Elon Howe, Rhoyda Maurer, Lester Maurer, Norman Maurer, Ruby Bidelman Wolever

The front and outer buildings of Thompson School

This essay was written by Norman Maurer (born Sept, 1909) in 1923 of 1924 when he was in the 8th grade at Thompson School.

The History of Big Prairie Township

The first settlers settled Big Prairie about 1850. They were Judge Barton, William Barton, Aaron Swain, George Utley, Henry French and a man called Dellzell. Henry French came from New York State. They settled on Big Prairie because the land was already cleared and there was plenty of timber in the county. They were mostly of Scottish, Irish and English descent. The first wedding was that of Theodore Taylor and Julia Swain. The first white child born on Big Prairie was Mr. McBridge. He lived two miles west of George Haight's corners in 1847.

Doctor Douglas Halton was an explorer of the Muskegon River. He sailed up the river in 1846.

The early settlers found the soil to be mostly a sandy loam and gravel. Their supply of water came from natural springs and dug wells. There was plenty of timber on Big Prairie Township, mostly oak, pine, beech, birch and elm. There was plenty of fish in the Muskegon River. Transportation was done by horse and wagon in the old days, but now we have auto trucks.

There was an Indian trail beginning at the river which ran across sections 16, 15, 10, 11, 2, 1. There was another trail across sections 27, 26, 23, 24. It was called the Canada trail because it was used by teamsters and lumbermen going to Canada for work. There were a number of corduroy roads in the township. Fifty six rods of corduroy road south of the Westcott place, was built for 66 cents per cord. Now most of the corduroy roads are graveled.

The first bridge in the township was built in 1877. It was called Whitney Bridge because it touched upon Robert Whitney's land. William Westcott drew the first load of lumber to make the bridge with. It was bought from J. M. Carr at Brady Lake, then the nearest saw mill.

The chief industries of the early settlers was lumbering and farming. A few taverns were found on the trails. One of these was Mitchell's Tavern located on the south east corner of section 24. The first lumber camp was owned by Mr. Black.

The people marketed their crops with horses, oxen and mules. There were no stage coaches used in this township.

Barn raising was a time of pleasure in the old days. The frame work of the sides and ends were nailed together and then the men raised them up and put them on a foundation. After the work was done they generally had a party and a dance in the new barn.

The first saw mill was owned by Ephraim Utley and the first grist mill was at Croton.

The first railroad was opened in 1868 and it ran from Muskegon to Big Rapids.

The first school house was built two miles west of Big Prairie Store and it was used for a church and a school and was called Union School.

The first church in District 10 was conducted by Elder Kelly and Elder Inman, both members of the Wesleyan Methodist Church. The first school house in district 10 (Thompson) was built in 1896 and stood just south of the cement building. It was made of log. The first teacher, Miss Mattie Voase who taught two terms. The present building was built 17 years ago and the first teacher was Miss Blanche Carr.

The first township officers were John Bety and William Utley. John Bety was elected supervisor and William Utley as clerk of Big Prairie. Mr. Swain was the first postmaster. The first post office was at Cox's corners. Mail was only carried from Croton on horseback but sometimes Mr. Elmer French carried it on foot. The leading party has been the Republican Party. On the farms the people raised wheat, millet, corn and oats. Wheat often brought forty bushel to the acre. Millet often brought $60 per ton.

Henry Barton, son of Judge Barton, was an officer in the Civil War. Three young men of the township gave their lives in the World War. They were Harold Schowmaker, Clyde Crabtree and Marshall Webster.

The scenery of the township is along the Muskegon River the ox bow and the white rollaways.

Richard Westgate memories:

Richard Westgate, son of Edgar and Hazel Westgate, lived on 32nd Street and attended during the 1920s through 1930s. His teachers were Don Jeffries and Mr. Ewing. Children he recalls attending: Harry, Harlan and Opal Dekker, Lester, Thelma and Norman Maurer, Melvin Weeks, Charlie, Alice and Stella Graves, Lucy Parrott, J.C. Howe, and Marian, Dick and Basil Westgate.

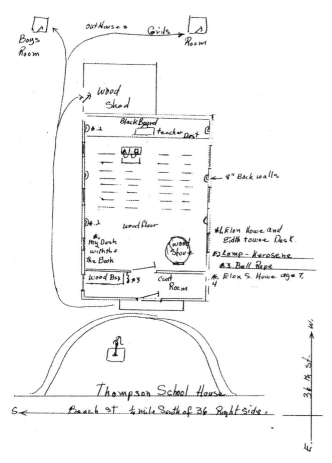

The layout of
Thompson School

Elon Howe memories:

Elon Stuart Howe lived on 32nd Street, the son of Joseph and Dorothy (Harris) Howe, when he attended Thompson School. He attended one year as a kindergartner from 1937 thru 1938. His lunch sandwiches were of beans or oleo on homemade bread. After lunch, there was a 30 minute recess and they tried to play softball. He recalls a picnic on the last day of school and the students went to the John Ball Zoo in Grand Rapids by bus. Ruth Maile was his teacher that year. There were outhouses in use. He states that the school consolidated with Morley School in 1938. Students that Elon went to school with in 1937-1938: Charles Parrott, Hilda Weeks, Jack Schoomaker, Lucie Linzie, Kenneth Towne, Ruth Schoomaker, Arthur Westgate, Edwin Towne, Cecil Decker, June Decker, Donald Howe, Donald Westgate, Vera Howe, Edith Towne, Christina McIntire, Evelyn McIntire.

A story related to Elon Howe is that when he was a young boy, the school house was also used for church services. Elon and his family attended the services there and it wasn't until he got a little older did he realize that the picture hanging on the wall was not Jesus but was George Washington.

Ruth Forwood Maile

Ruth Forwood Maile was born Sept. 27, 1896 at the corner of Elm and 20th Street in Big Prairie Township. She graduated from Howard City High School and then attended County Normal in Fremont to obtain a teaching certificate. Ruth and her husband Elmer Maile raised three children. She taught school for over 30 years. Most of these years were spent in one room school houses. Wages were sometimes $30 a month and she had to build the fires when needed. Before she married she had her own horse to travel to and from school. These are some of the schools she taught at: a school in Big Prairie Twp Sec. 15, Thompson School in Sec. 26 of Big Prairie Twp, Tripp School in Sec. 36 of Everett Twp, Fetterly School in Sec. 15 of Goodwell Twp, Croton School in Croton, and also a school in Schoolcraft and Morley Michigan.

Ruth (Forwood) Maile

Thompson School sudents circa 1938
Front row: Arthur Westgate, Edwin Towne, Cecil Decker, June Decker, Donald Howe, Elon Howe, Donald Westgate
Back row: Charles Parrott, Hilda Weeks, Jack Schoomaker, Lucy Parrott, Kenneth Towne, Ruth Schoomaker, Teacher Ruth Maile

Thompson School students circa 1925
Front row: Unknown, Basil Westgate
Back row: Unknown, Arthur Westcott, unknown, unknown, Thelma Maurer

Basil Westgate is on the shoulders
of Arthur Westcott. The girl in back
is Thelma Maurer. The building
is the woodshed behind Thompson
School.

Thompson School students circa 1939
Front row: Jack Schoomaker and Kenneth Towne (1st and 2nd from left)
Back row: Rhoyda Maurer (last on right in black jacket)

Charles Parrott memories:

Charles Parrott, son of Lee and Pearl Parrott, attended Thompson School while living on Beech Street. He typically walked home for lunch and recalls playing ball and tag and also in a sand pile on the playground. There were outhouses used and recalls having Ruth Maile, Don Jeffers and Mr. Ewing as teachers. He rode a school bus when he went to public school.

Brooks Township

Brooks Township was one of the original two townships of Newaygo County established in 1851 and comprised the western half of the county. Brooks Township's area was reduced over the years to make way for new townships. The 1880 plat map shows the township as being the east half of what is now Garfield (Garfield Township did not exist yet) and the west half of the current Brooks Township. The east half of what is currently Brooks Township was part of Croton Township at that time. The map only shows one country school in Brooks Township, located in Section 11 of what is now Garfield Township. In 1881 it was established as the township area that it is known as today (Township 12 North, Range 12 West).

Information on the early schools of Brooks Township is scarce. Mostly likely, the majority of students in the township lived close enough to town to attend Newaygo Public Schools. In 1883, there is a reference that Brooks Township had four school districts with three frame schoolhouses and one log schoolhouse.

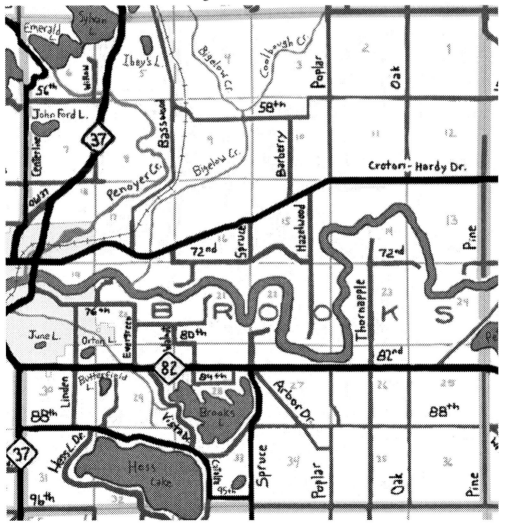

1900

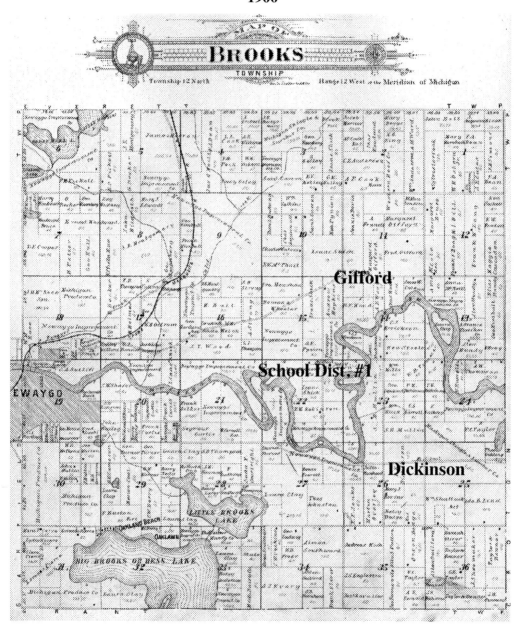

1922

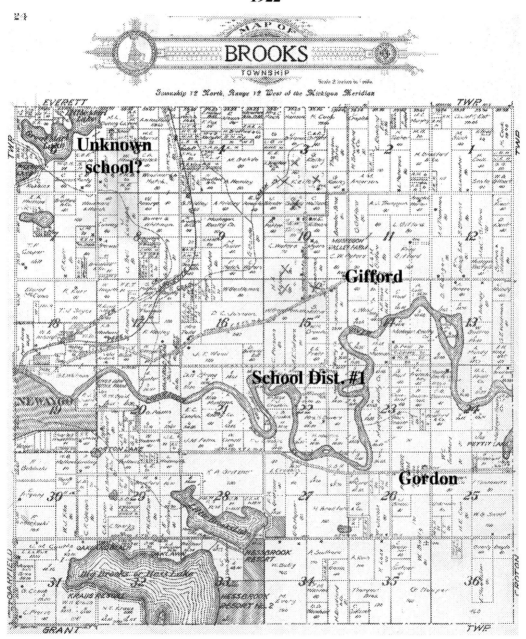

School District #1
Section 22 - 72nd Street

This school apparently did not have a proper name, it was just known as School District #1. The only information that could be found on this school is its location at the corner of Hazelwood and 72nd Street. It had closed by 1941.

Unknown School
Section 5

There is a school shown on the 1922 plat map near Little Marl Lake, but the name of the school has not been found and no other information is known about this school.

SATISFACTION

There's no thrill in easy sailing when
  the skies are clear and blue,
There's no joy in merely doing things
  that any one can do,
But there is some satisfaction that is
  mighty sweet to take,
When you reach a destination that
  you thought you'd never make.

So when everything's against you and
  your plans are going wrong,
Just face the situation and keep
  moving right along—
Don't sit down and wail and whimper,
  even though you may be stuck,
You're not absolutely helpless if you
  still possess your pluck.

Inspirational Poster No. 37

Gifford School

Gifford School
AKA Pink School
School District #3

Gifford School, also known as Pink School, was located on Croton Road, 5 or 6 miles east of Newaygo between Poplar and Oak Avenues in Section 11. At one time, it had been located about one mile north of that location. Pink School was in session in 1895.

Gifford School was built about 1900 on one acre of the property that Walter Gifford bought. The school remained on Croton Road until the early 1950's when it was replaced by a home. It was a one room school with a separate wood shed in back along with two out-houses. A large pot bellied wood stove kept the students partly warm during cold weather. Students sat on bench type seats, two students to each bench, facing the teacher. Generally, there were about 12 students total for the whole school, including all eight grades with only one teacher. The drinking water came from a common pail that students filled each morning by pumping water, by hand, from a well about 50 feet from the school.

The 1933 school records show that there were 22 students attending this school. In 1938, there were 18 students attending.

In August of 1941, a note in the Newaygo Republican stated "Gifford School is the only rural school open in Brooks Township. Miss Edna Palarski is the teacher."

Gifford school was built around 1900.

Gifford school students in 1927 or 1928. The teacher, Miss Dodge, is second from the left in the back row. The Hoag children are in the back row (fourth and fifth from left) and Faye Evan Gifford is on the end in the front row.

11/1/1894 Newaygo Republican

The following is a report of School District #3 (Gifford School) in the Township of Brooks for the month ending 10/27/1894: Number of days taught 20. Number of pupils enrolled 17. Number of pupils enrolled 17. Pupils present every day: Grace Angevine, Jennie Delano, Harry Delano, Chancy Delano, Lee Force, Edith Race, Arthur Race, Albert Race, Frank Race, Anna McNeil, Otto Gifford, Clarence Gifford. Emma Thompson, Teacher.

Memories of Fay Gifford

Gifford school was a one-room school where Margaret, Doris and Fay Gifford attended school grades one through eight. One teacher taught all eight grades in all the subjects. The total number of students was generally around a dozen. Outhouses were out in back of the school along with a woodshed. A hand pumped well furnished drinking and washing water. Kerosene lamps hung on the wall and furnished light in the dark winter months. We took turns raising and lowering the American flag when the weather was decent.

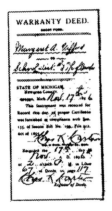

This is a page copied from the Gifford family history book written by Fay Gifford

This legal document shows that Margaret (Spoor) Gifford signed over one acre of her property to a local school district in Newaygo County in 1896 for $20. The one room school built on this one acre was known as the Gifford School.

Gordon School
School District #4
AKA Dickinson School
School District #5
AKA Ewing School

No photographs of this school, which has changed names and school district numbers throughout the years, have been located. Prior to 1880, the school was located in Croton Township, which at that time extended into the east half of what is currently Brooks Township.

It was most likely first known as the Ewing School and may have been located in Section 25.

On March 23, 1877, Philip Dickinson and his wife, Sophronia, sold to School District #5 of Croton Township (what is now Brooks Township) one acre of land for the sum of $15. This was near the corners of sections 23, 24, 25 and 26. The road is now M-82 on the edge of Surrerar Prairie. The previous school had been located one mile south near the Surrerar Cemetery.

The school sometimes was referred to as Surrerar Prairie School. A June 20, 1895 Newaygo Republican article gives a school report for Surrerar Prairie School for month ending June 6. Pupils enrolled: 15. Neither absent nor tardy: Carrie, Esther and Earl Mills. Pupils standing highest in scholarship: Will Cudihy 86, Carrie Taylor 82, Roy Dickinson 77. Nettie Gifford, Teacher.

Eight grades of school were held at Dickinson School until 1925 when the remaining students were transported to the City of Newaygo where a new school was being built.

Mr. and Mrs. Dickinson lived on the prairie until the Gordon family moved there in about 1919. The Gordon School, mostly likely named after the Gordon family, was located on Oak Avenue between 82nd and 88th Streets in Section 26.

In 1933 Gordon School had 13 students attending and by 1938 there were only 10. The school had closed by 1941.

Croton Township

Croton Township was created in 1855 and included all of the 12 mile square area of land in the county's southeast corner. By 1881, Croton Township was reduced to its final shape. It is designated at Township 12 North, Range 11 West.

In 1880, the township had four whole school districts and two fractional school districts with all being framed buildings. There were 166 students attending school with four male teachers and seven female teachers. Wages ranged from $573 for male teachers to $672.60 for female teachers.

1900

1922

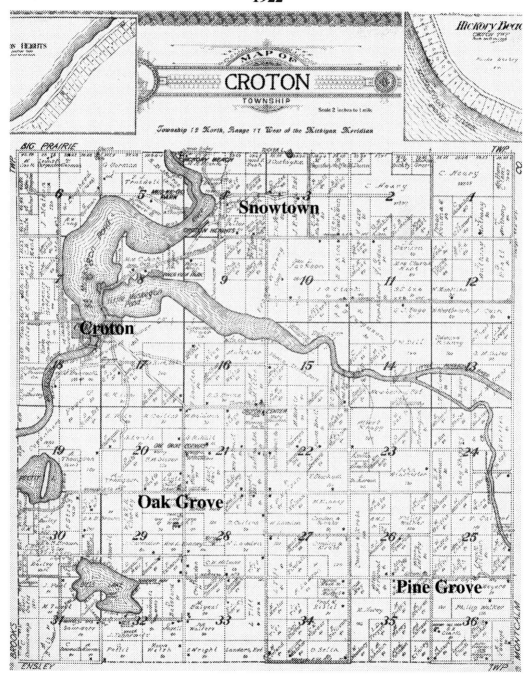

Christian Plains School

Christian Plains School was located on the northwest corner of Section 22 at the corner of 72nd and Cottonwood. It was one of the early schools that closed at the end of the logging era.

Lillie Newberg, daughter of Matts and Maximillia, was born in 1891. She attended the Kinney School, and later went to Ferris State College where she earned her right to teach school. In 1910 she taught school at the Christian Plains School in Croton Township. It was a one-room school and she taught all seven grades. There were 13 students in all. While teaching at this school she boarded with the George Merrifield family. In this way she met Henry P. Merrifield, son of the George and Susie. Three of their girls attended this school. On July 2, 1911, she married Henry and they had six children.

Newaygo Republican exerpts:
January 1901 – "There will be an entertainment at the Christian Plains School House on Wednesday evening January 30."
April 7, 1903 – "Our new school bell is a reality, as it is on the road from Chicago now. The people of the school district ought to be able to build a cupola and hang the bell as it has cost them nothing to get it."
June 25, 1903 – "Did you hear our new school bell ring? Simon Dancer and Mr. Knapp put up the belfry Saturday and with the help of Robert Parrish, hung the bell.

Croton School
School District #2

Croton School was located in Section 8 in heart of Croton and was one of the earliest schools to open in Newaygo County. There were at least three schools built - two were wood structures and the last was a brick building. The annual Old Settlers picnic, which began about 1920, was often held at the Croton Schoolhouse.

Teachers for 1938-1940: Esther Wyss (teaching 1st, 2nd and 3rd grades), Ella Steinke (teaching 4th, 5th and 7th grades), and Arthur E. Salisbury (7th, 8th and 9th grades).

Report of Croton Township, School District 2, month ending May 31, 1895. 32 pupils enrolled. The following pupils were not absent: Berta Smith, Rossie Hinkson, Maude Race, Vera Gauweiler, Ina Grow, Ethel Race, Ernest Carpenter, Floyd Dancer, John Dancer, Ray Rice. Mamie Traver, Teacher.

In the Jan. 11, 1900 issue of the Newaygo Republican, Croton School is mentioned having 23 pupils enrolled with Esther Rice, Harry Rice, Carrie and Jerome Botsford, Bernice Merritt, Mary, Ada and Leonard Wells not absent or tardy.

For the month of November 1901, there were 24 students enrolled with Mary Wells, Leonard Wells, Carrie Botsford, Jerome Botsford, Ealease Botsford, Esther Rice and Harry Rice neither tardy or absent.

The "new" brick building Croton School

The old Croton Schoolhouse

Interior of the Croton School

Students outside of the second built Croton School

The Old Settler's Picnic was held at the Croton School

Croton School 1938 Students
Front row: *Robert Plank, Daisy Moore, Jack duChemin, Elmer Parcher, Gerald*
  Fry, ? Stephenson, David(?) Davidson, Ralph Plank, Loretta Maurer Bisel,
  Memory Kent, Ruby Davis Gilewski, unknown, Robert Christner, Howard
  Widmeyer, Earl Ronning, Charles Blok, Jean Maile Blackall, Elmo Davidson,
  Howard Sullivan
Middle row: *Robert Carpenter, Wesley Stephenson, Margaret Jump Staples, Marilyn*
  Stephenson, Mable Blok, Mary Lou Johnson, Lloyd Davidson, Joe Maile, Ed
  duChemin, Nora Haight, Jim Sullivan, Leo Christner, June Hickman, Eva
  Jean Widmeyer, Sylvia Stephenson, Lucille Hooker, Chet O'Neil, Grace
  Westcott, Leola Lorenz, Joan Kent, Mary Quackenbush, Iola Lorenz, Dale
  Dunlap, Lola Biggs Cronk, Russel Ronning
Back row: *Tom O'Neil, Jack Sturtevant, Raymond Fry, Bill Corbin, Louis Laidley,*
  Evadine Davidson, Evelyn Westcott, Margie Davidson Thomas, Rose
  Burnham, Mary Goodenuff, Dorothy Sullivan, Richard Dykeman, Clare
  Walters Jr., Buster Hickman (Edmund), Bert Sullivan, Bill Hofferd, Bernice
  Young, Christine Robinson, teacher Arthur Salisbury, Alice Haight, Bonnie
  Young Sturtevant, Maxine Peters, Irene Peters, Bob Hickman, Ellis Salisbury,
  Richard Corbin, Robert Young, teacher Miss Steinke, Robert Bader,
  teacher Miss Wyss

1938 Croton School students - Teacher Miss Fox
Front row: Don Strohpaul, Gerald Fry, Howard Widmayor
Middle row: Memory Kent, Daisey Moore, unknown, Sylvia Stephson, unknown,
*   unknown, unknown, Earl (Johnny) Roning, Loretta Maurer Bisel*
Back row: Marilyn Stephson, Robert Plank, Howard Sulivan, Margeret Jump
*   Staples, Lloyd Davidson, Joe Maile, Ed duChemin, Mable Blok, Elmo*
*   Davidson, Jean Maile Blackall, Bob Christenson, Charles Blok*

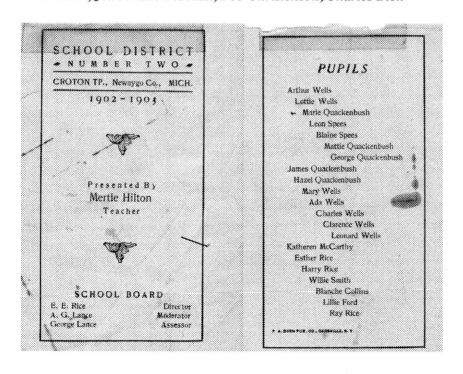

SCHOOL DISTRICT
• NUMBER TWO •
CROTON TP., Newaygo Co., MICH.
1902 - 1903

Presented By
Mertie Hilton
Teacher

SCHOOL BOARD
E. E. Rice   Director
A. G. Lance   Moderator
George Lance   Assessor

PUPILS
Arthur Wells
Lottie Wells
Marie Quackenbush
Leon Spees
Blaine Spees
Mattie Quackenbush
George Quackenbush
James Quackenbush
Hazel Quackenbush
Mary Wells
Ada Wells
Charles Wells
Clarence Wells
Leonard Wells
Katheren McCarthy
Esther Rice
Harry Rice
Willie Smith
Blanche Collins
Lillie Ford
Ray Rice

1946 Croton School students - Teacher Nellie Beduhn
Front row: Edna duChemin, Shirley Lorenze, Margaret Maurer Holmes, Bonnie
Gruenberg, unknown, Florence Davidson, Ida Moore, Daisy Moore
Back row: Melvin Moore, Carl Gruenberg, Donald Jones, unknown, Ira Burnham,
Roger Cole, Gib Mara, D.O. Barton, unknown, Grant Bisel, Ernie
Gruenberg, Richard Maurer

1946 Croton School students - Teacher Ruth Maile
Front row: Harry Weimer, Ned Bisel, Mike Weimer, unknown, unknown, unknown,
Sharron Westoctt, Lorena Gruenberg, unknown
Back row: unknown, Judy Aiken, Edith Aish, Billie McAvoy, Anna McAvoy, Bert
Jones, Arthur Westcott, unknown, unknown, Blair Cole, Marvin Davidson,
Orville Westcott, unknown, Bruce Barton

1946-1947 Croton School students Teacher - Nellie Beduhn Front row: Blair Cole, unknown, Billie McAvoy, Sonya Stebbing Cool, unknown, unknown, Bruce Barton, unknown, Donald Jones

Middle row: Orville Westcott, Arthur Westcott, unknown, Bonnie Gruenberg, Grant Bisel, unknown, Bert Jones

Back row: unknown, Marvin Davidson, Ira Burnham, unknown, Al Weimer, Larry Cornelious, Carl Gruenberg

Circa 1938 Croton School Band Members
Left to right: Herman Christian, Rosie Burnham, Leola Lorenz, Lucille Hooker, Dale Dunlap, John Davidson, Clifford Branch (teacher), Eva Jean Widmeyer Osborn, Iola Lorenz, Joan Kent, Bert Sullivan, Dorothy Sullivan, Ed duChemin, Joe Maile, Mary Ellen Goodenuff, Wesley Stephenson, Mary Jane Quackenbush, Doris Strohpaul Bush, Doris Strohpaul Purcell, Buster Hickman, Margie Davidson Thomas, Lola Jane Biggs Cronk, Bill Hofferd, Bill Corbin, Bonnie Young Sturtevant, Chet O'Neil, Stella Church, Mary Young, Bob Hickman

Croton School 1947-1948 1st, 2nd and 3rd Grades - Teacher Ruth Maile
Front row: Leroy Aishe, Lorena Gruenberg, unknown, ? Laneski, Dick Shaffer,
     unknown, unknown, Judy Aiken
2nd row: Sharron Westcott, Ronald Towne, Sandra Corbin, unknown, Danny
     Stebing, unknown, unknown, Merril Maurer, Eva ?, Mary Fredenburg
3rd row: Sarah McEvoy, Carl Burnham, Karen Mudget, Ivan Sperry, Doreen Marsh,
     Harry Weimer
Back row: Judy Mudget, teacher Ruth Maile, Dorothy Siefma, Mary Towne Ogg,
     Doreen ?, Ned Bisel, Myron Weimer, Billy Gregg, unknown

Croton School 1957-1958
Kindergarten Class

Carl Van Oss, Joan "Skeeter"
Maurer, teacher Ruth Maile,
Ben Moose, Janet Hulst, Fred
Davidson

Croton School students circa 1932
Front row: #3 John Davidson; #5 Bob Young
Back row: #2 Jack Sturtevant; #9 Esther Wyss, teacher

1939-1940 Croton Dancers
Iris Tift is the fourth from left; Jean Maile Blackall and Joe Maile are holding Cro-
ton banners, girl on Joe's right is Mable Blok. center girl is June Hickman (check-
ered skirt), to her left is Iola Lorenz and to her right are Lucille Hooker, Lola Biggs
Cronk and Mary Jane Quackenbush; from the right - #2 Loretta Maurer Bisel; #4
Mary Lou Johnson; #5 Edmund duChemin, #7 Micky Ledega, #8 Joann Roby.

Early Croton School students

PROGRAM

PROCESSIONAL .... Mrs. Peggy Salisbury

INVOCATION .... Rev. David Mills
First Baptist Church, Newaygo

CLASS HISTORY .... Cathy Jo Maile
CO-SALUTATORIAN .... Debbie Miller
CO-SALUTATORIAN ...... Janet Howarth

CLASS WILL ...... Robert Davison, John Nitz

GIFTATORY .... Linda Bisel, Debra Smith

CLASS ADDRESS .... Dolores Toth
VALEDICTORIAN

SCHOOL CHOIR, Mrs. Frances Branyan, Dir.

ADDRESS .... Mr. Victor Sisung
Guidance Counselor, Newaygo High School

AWARDS .... Mr. Ralph LeBlanc, Principal

DIPLOMAS .... Mr. Don Rathbun, Supt.

BENEDICTION .... Rev. David Mills

Croton School Graduation Program

The Graduating Class of the
Croton Township Schools extend
to you a cordial invitation to
attend the Union Commencement
Exercises, Wednesday evening,
June sixteenth, nineteen hundred
and fifteen, at the M. E. church,
Oak Grove, at eight o'clock.

1915

Graduates

HELEN GROW
LENA WIES
CHARLIE WRIGHT
CLARE DUNWORTH
FRED GAUWEILER
RALPH LOUDEN
ETHEL RICH
FLORENCE NORWOOD

Teachers

INEZ MELLON   F. E. HICKS
RUTH HOARE
MRS. ALFRED JOHNSON

Class Motto—Discouragement is Un-American
Class Colors—Green and White
Class Flower—White Rose

Program

March		
Invocation	. . .	Rev. Carl Wilt
Music	. . .	Oak Grove Quartette
Address	. .	Rev. J. F. Bowerman
Violin Solo	. . .	Thomas Collins
Presentation of Diplomas		Isabelle M. Becker
		Com. of Schools
Vocal Solo	. . .	Mrs. C. G. Larry
Benediction	. . .	Rev. Carl Wilt

Baccalaureate Sermon, Sunday evening,
1915 June 13, by Rev. Carl Wilt

Croton School 1940-41 9th Grade Class
Left to right: Robert Young Leola Lorenz, Charles Tawney, Richard Corbin,
Maryjane Quackenbush, Evadene Davision, Carolyn Truesdell, Dorothy Sullivan

Croton School 1940-41 9th Grade girls
Left to right: Leola Lorenz, Evadene Davison, Maryjane Quackenbush,
Dorothy Sullivan and Carolyn Truesdell

Croton School Students 1947-48
4th, 5th & 6th Grades - Teacher: Nellie Beduhn
Seated: ? Weimer, Blair Cole, Marvin Davidson, Bruce Barton, Melvin Moore,
    unknown, Carl Gruenberg, Grant Bisel, unknown, unknown, Ira Burnham,
    Lillian MacAvoy, Anna Bell Macavoy
Standing: Roger Cole, Margaret Maurer Holmes, Shirley Lorenze, D.O. Barton,
    Evan Billings, Floyd Towne

Oak Grove School

Oak Grove School
School District #3

In 1988 the Michigan Historical Commission listed Oak Grove #3 School House in the State Register of Historic Sites. The school house is located five miles south of Croton on the corner of Elm and 80th Street in Section 20.

The 3 R's were very important to the pioneer parents of the Croton area. Men and women of this time era worked very hard and together in helping one another in social get-togethers called "bees." It took many hands and animals to cut trees, remove stumps, and make land tillable.

A log school house was erected around 1861 and also became the neighborhood meeting house. School terms were short compared to the present day allowing children to be involved in seasonal chores. The average wage for a teacher was from $3.00 to $5.00 per week and "board around." A record of the Oak Grove School can be found in the archives of the State Department in Lansing that states that in the 1870's, Oak Grove had the largest library of the six public schools in Croton Township. Three schools had no books at all.

The site where the first Oak Grove school house was built was a donation from Henry Utley in 1861. School was first held in the Old White Church across from the cemetery. James Biggs took the contract to build the school house, furnish the material and do all the work for $175.00. A man named Ambrose took the job of building the woodshed and furnishing all the material for $10.00. Susan Dalziel was the first teacher. There were 14 scholars who received certificates and taught successful schools without going to high school. They were 2 Swains, 6 Utleys, 6 Bartons, William Doyle, and Avarilda Cain.

There was a meeting with Mrs. Mina Utley to make the school banner. The next thing to do was to choose a name for the school house. With one vote everyone said "Utley," but Henry Utley came in and vetoed that by saying emphatically "No!" Someone suggested the name "Oak Grove" school, Big Prairie. All agreed. The old school banner was kept in the Swain house until it was put in the refuse heap.

Oak Grove paid out $2.65 in repairs in 1870. Property taxes on 80 acres were between $6.00 and $7.00 in 1869. The people gathered at the school house on Sunday to hear Elder Somebody preach. There they sang familiar hymns with wind and birds to accompany them. Here the young people had "spell downs" and "cipher downs."

The children enjoyed playing many different games on the playground: Fox and Geese, tag, jacks, throwing balls, pom pom pull away, jump rope, red rover, softball, crack the whip, marbles, dodgeball, climbing apple trees, chase the boys, slide, teeter totter, rings and maypole. The Christmas programs were held in the church which was next door to the school They also had other social events call "Mayday," "Penny Suppers," and "Box Socials."

At that time, the Muskegon River was the main means of travel, first by the Indians and then by white men. The source of the river is Houghton Lake. Where Croton village now stands, was named Muskegon Forks because of the meeting of the Big and Little Muskegon rivers. No bridge or dam troubled the flow of the unpolluted waters. Muskegon was then a small town on Lake Michigan. Grand Rapids was a village on the Grand River and was about 80 miles south of Croton. It took three days to go to Muskegon by canoe or flatboat. These two villages were the nearest points of supplies. The Indians were friendly and often assisted the white men in hauling supplies.

The school house burned down about 1914. A brick school house was built in 1915 after schools in the area consolidated due to the increase in population as a result of the construction of the Croton Dam in 1906. Oak Grove #3 housed grades Kindergarten through 8th grade from 1915 until 1968, when declining enrollment forced its closure.

The school is a gable-roofed brick building resting on a fieldstone foundation. A projecting pavilion frames the round, arched entrance, which is flanked by one story, hip-roofed wings. The school is crowned by a pyramidal-roofed, hexagonal cupola. The old building is now owned by Pam Greinke. She and Tom Thompson have brought the structure back from disrepair while keeping it as original as possible.

Oak Grove School

Oak Grove school and church

Oak Grove Teachers: Ethel Sullivan (Feb. 1895), Miss Leman (1902), Pearl Harrison (1901-1902), Miss Daugherty (1902), Olive Forwood (1910), Abbie Gale Nelson (1938, 1940), Ray Kludy (1938, 1941), Susan Dalziel, Olive Forwood, Hannah Wenstrom, Mildred Dodge, Clair Dunworth, Margaret Anderson, Beatrice Bryant, Mrs. Gorby, Mr. Johnson, Joy Brisbin, Doreen Allen, Jean Bergman, Earl Page.

Oak Grove School report for month ending May 10, 1887. Number of pupils enrolled 45. Average standings for the month: Myra Bills 91; Willie VanLieu 87; Ralph Collins 81; Hattie Hall 92; Edna Parks 84; Angie Hart 76; Maud Harrison 85; Libbie Dancer 92; Cassie Miller 91; Guy Wright 80; Elsie Hanson 85; Zoe Bennett 89; Lela Cram 90; George VanLieu 85; Rosa Miller 91; Ethel Collins 89; Emma Miller 91; Etha Huested 88; Ella Miller 91; Edith Dancer 80; Bell Harrison 86; Glen Harrison 90. Pupil having greatest number head marks: B Class - Rosa Miller; C Class - Pearl Harrison. Ann Gorman was the teacher.

1898 Oak Grove School graduate - Christina Grace Cavender

Oak Grove 8th grade graduates in May 1937: Vera May Thompson, Margery Stray, Harold Grant and Jack Friend; 10th grade graduates: Crystene Lentz, Crystal Lentz and Rex Medaris

Newaygo Republican excerpts:
December 13, 1894 – Report of Oak Grove School, District #3, Croton Township, for the term ending 11/23/1894. Boys enrolled 19 and girls enrolled 23. Name of pupil not absent: Irma Keeney. H. Hornbeck, Teacher
January 3, 1901 – Mrs. Belle Pellit buys a library for her school District #4 Croton. We are sure that this will prove a blessing to the little people in that section.
December 1901 - 27 pupils enrolled for the month of November. Students who never tardy were Hazel Harrison, Charlie Harrison, Edna Parish, Olai Parish. Scholars never absent were Angeline Aldridge, Belle Tracy, Olai Parish, Edna Seeners.
February 6, 1902 – Oak Grove School closed Feb. 4 with Miss Leman as teacher, but will commence again on Feb. 18 with our old teacher Miss Dorety [Daugherty].
March 13, 1902 – Oak Grove School closed for 2-3 weeks on account of smallpox.
May 13, 1948 – "On Friday, May 14, the pupils of Oak Grove School will travel to Lansing, where they expect to visit the capital building. In recognition of Mother's Day and the mothers of Oak Grove District, the pupils presented a program where each mother received a corsage. Helen Wright is president of the club."
May 20, 1948 – Oak Grove children enjoyed a picnic last week. School was closed for the summer vacation yesterday.

Memories of Vera M. Thompson Shutts

Vera Thompson Shutts attended Oak Grove School from Kindergarten to 10th grade (1928-1939). Her parents, Archie and Ruth Thompson, lived on Locust Street. Her lunch consisted of a sandwich, cake, orange, tomato and a boiled egg. Typical games played were Fox and Geese, tag, and jacks. Most memorable school event was the Christmas program. Vera remembers that the school had both outdoor and indoor bathrooms. Kindergarten through fifth grade students were seated on the west side of the school and faced north while sixth through 10th grades were seated on the east side and faced south.

Vera's teachers were Mildred Dodge, Clare Dunworth and Ray Kludy. One teacher, Ruth (Thompson) Asprey, boarded with Vera's family.

Some of the students Vera remembers attending Oak Grove School were: Students who attended Oak Grove School: Forrest, Mary, Flossie, Kenneth, Luella, Ron and Don Shutts; Connie, Dale, and Phil Thompson; Earl, Elaine, Louis, Richard Derwin; Hazel, Richard, Norma, and Arthur Mosher; Merrill, Louise, Margery, and Frankie Stray; Ruth, Clara, Eleanor, and John Stray; Margaret, Luella, and Marie Shutts; Lawrence, Norman, Beulah, Vernon, and Harold Wright; Marion, Lila, Dorothy, and Beatrice Skinner

Vera rode a bus to Howard City to attend high school. She graduated in 1941.

"I think the original school house burned down in 1919 or before. The kids went to school in the church next door until the brick school house was built.

"My Dad, Archie Thompson, and his two brothers, Francis and Harold, went to school in the original wood building.

"When the basement for the new brick building was dug, Herman Shaw, pushed Harold Thompson down in the hold. Harold's left leg was injured and never grew, or not much after that. He used a crutch to walk for the rest of his life. He was born in 1907 and I always heard he was 12 years old when that happened. He lived to be 62-1/2 years old."

Memories of Debbie (Thompson) Deuling

Debbie Thompson Deuling attended Oak Grove School from Kindergarten in 1963 until the school closed due to consolidation (about 1965). Her lunches consisted of peanut butter and jelly sandwiches and cookies. Recess games included pom-pom pull away and Red Rover. She also remembered climbing and playing under the apple trees. The special event of the year was the Christmas program. Debbie remembers practicing at the church located next door to the school. She also remembers that Miss Arnold and Miss Enzer came to lead Bible Club and that her dad said that "they came when I was in school."

The school's indoor bathrooms were located on each side of the stair well to the basement. Students in Kindergarten through fourth grade sat in rows in the "little room" and the fifth through eight graders were seated in the "big room."

"The milk was kept in the basement and the 'milk helpers' got to go get it and pass it out each day." The students were given white milk Monday through Thursday and chocolate milk on Friday.

Debbie's teacher was Mrs. Bergman and other student family names were: Crawford, Dietz, Toth, Scutter, Westgate, Rank, Wright, Force (Nancy and Sally) and Anderson.

Memories of Margaret (Shutts) Thomas

Margaret Shutts lived on E. 76th Street with her parents, Leonard and Ruth (Stray) Shutts. She attended Oak Grove School from Kindergarten through seventh grade (1936 to 1944). She remembers that her noon time lunch contained a sandwich, cake, and an apple or pear. At recess, the kids played ball, tag, Pom Pom pull away and jump rope. Special programs were May Day and at Christmas.

Margaret's teachers were Margaret Anderson, Abigail Nelson, Ray Kludy and Beatrice Bryant. Other students who attended the school were: Mary Ann and Bernice Brooks; Jim, Marjorie, Raymond, and Lester Wright; Arthur, Evan, and Leon Billings; Imogene and Iris Tift; Margaret, Luella and Marie Shutts; Earl, Elaine and Louis Derwin; Arthur and Norma Mosher; and Connie, Dale and Phillip Thompson.

Memories of Roberta Crain Weaver

Roberta Crain Weaver and her parents, Roblee and Burnette, lived on Cypress Street when Roberta attended Oak Grove School from Kindergarten through sixth grade (1954 to 1961). Lunch consisted of a sandwich and either fruit or cake. Typical games played were Red Rover, softball, crack the whip, marbles and dodge ball. The Christmas plays were always a special event.

Roberta's teachers were Mrs. Gorby, Mrs. Allen, Miss Brisbee and Mr. Johnson. Students she remembers attended Oak Grove were: Carol, Paul, and Nancy Coons; Sherry, Beverly, Cleta, Norris, and Victor Wright; Roger and Linda Quick; Carol Reed; Jean Ellen Stray; Gary Emory, Eilene, Leo, and Charlene Wright; Steven, Jim, Danny, Rebecca, Eunice, and Faith Bunker; and Carl Dosch.

Memories of Robin (Thomas) Phillips

Robin Thomas attended Oak Grove School from Kindergarten through sixth grade (1959 to 1965). She and her parents, Ernest and Margaret (Shutts) Thomas, lived on Elm Ave. Special events included penny suppers and the Christmas program. Robin's teachers included Joy Brisbin, Doreen Allen, Jean Bergman, and Earl Page. Joanne Toth and Marilyn Dietz also attended Oak Grove School.

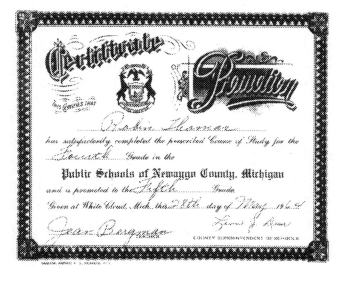

NEWAYGO COUNTY PUBLIC SCHOOLS
Report of Pupil's Progress

Name _Robin Thomas_

Grade _1st_ Promoted to grade _2nd_

School _Oak Grove_

School Year 19_60_ to 19_61_

Teacher _Mrs. Miller_

* Parent's Signature

1. _Mrs. Ernest Thomas_
2. _Ernest Thomas_
3. _Ernest Thomas_
   Ernest Thomas
   Ernest Thomas
6. ....

*Note: Your signature means only that you have seen the card.

TO PARENTS: It is the purpose of our schools to have your child enjoy his education, and to have him develop and grow steadily, not only in mind, but in character as well. We must remember that children need to learn, not only subject matter, but also how to live together and become good citizens.

Providing a child with an education is a community undertaking. The home must share with the school the responsibility for developing desirable traits of character and proper attitudes toward life. Your cooperation will be appreciated by the teachers and they will be glad to discuss with you concerning your child's progress.

LEON J. DEUR,
County School Superintendent

NEWAYGO COUNTY PUBLIC SCHOOLS
Report of Pupil's Progress

Name _Robin Thomas_

Grade _3_ Promoted to grade _4_

School _Oak Grove_

School Year 19_62_ to 19_63_

Teacher _Mrs. Jean Bergman_

* Parent's Signature

1. _Mrs. Ernest Thomas_
2. _Ernest Thomas_
3. _Mrs. Ernest Thomas_
4. _Ernest Thomas_
5. _Mrs. Ernest Thomas_
6. ....

*Note: Your signature means only that you have seen the card.

TO PARENTS: It is the purpose of our schools to have your child enjoy his education, and to have him develop and grow steadily, not only in mind, but in character as well. We must remember that children need to learn, not only subject matter, but also how to live together and become good citizens.

Providing a child with an education is a community undertaking. The home must share with the school the responsibility for developing desirable traits of character and proper attitudes toward life. Your cooperation will be appreciated by the teachers and they will be glad to discuss with you concerning your child's progress.

LEON J. DEUR,
County School Superintendent

NEWAYGO COUNTY PUBLIC SCHOOLS
Report of Pupil's Progress

Name _Elizabeth Crawford_

Grade _K_ Promoted to grade _1_

School _Oak Grove_

School Year 19_62_ to 19_63_

Teacher _Mrs. Jean Bergman_

* Parent's Signature

1. ....
2. ....
3. _Mrs. Harry Crawford_
4. ....
5. _Mrs. Harry Crawford_
6. ....

*Note: Your signature means only that you have seen the card.

TO PARENTS: It is the purpose of our schools to have your child enjoy his education, and to have him develop and grow steadily, not only in mind, but in character as well. We must remember that children need to learn, not only subject matter, but also how to live together and become good citizens.

Providing a child with an education is a community undertaking. The home must share with the school the responsibility for developing desirable traits of character and proper attitudes toward life. Your cooperation will be appreciated by the teachers and they will be glad to discuss with you concerning your child's progress.

LEON J. DEUR,
County School Superintendent

RATINGS

A—Does very good work
B—Does well, above average
C—Does as well as average
D—Below average
E—Failure
I—Incomplete

SUBJECTS	1ST SEMESTER					2ND SEMESTER				
	1	2	3	EXM	SEM AV.	1	2	3	EXM	SEM AV.
Arithmetic	C	A			B	B	B+	B+		B+
Arts	C	C	B		B	B	B	B		B
English										
History										
Health										
Penmanship	C	C				C	C+	B-		C+
pre Reading	B-	B				C	B-	B+		B-
Spelling										
Geography										
Science										
Civics & Current Events										
Music										
Days Absent							1			
Times Tardy										

Memories of Iris L. (Tift) Davidson

Iris (Tift) Davidson attended Oak Grove School from Kindergarten through third grade (1936 to 1940). She and her parents, Harold and Mabel Tift, lived at M-46 and Cypress.

Iris' lunch usually consisted of a peanut butter sandwich, an apple and a cookie. Recess time was spent chasing the boys and playing on the slide, teeter totter, rings, and May Pole.

Memorable events were the box socials and Christmas programs.

Iris' teachers were Miss Anderson, Miss Nelson and Mr. Kludy. Other classmates were Margie, Jim Lester, Harold and Vernon Wright; Connie Thompson, Melvin McKinnon, Maxine Tawney, Richard Mosher, Lawrence and Beulah Wright, Ron Shutts, Imogene Boyd, Bob Storms, Imogene Tift, Mary Skinner, Norman Wright and Kenneth Boyd.

Iris Tift

Oak Grove 1939 Class - Teacher Abigail Nelson
Front row: Doris Boyd, Arthur Mosher, Vernon Wright, Louis Derwin, Ila Mae Holmes, Elaine Derwin, Luella Shutts
2nd row: Iris Tift, Marjory Wright, Harold Wright, Jim Wright, Earl Derwin, Connie Thompson, Mary Ann Brock, Judy Nelson, Norma Boyd, Margaret Shutts
Back row: Charles Nelson, Norman Wright, Bob Martin, Imogene Tift, Beulah Wright

Oak Grove Class
Front row: Melvin McKinnon, Mary Ann Brock, Jim Wright, Iris Tift, Harold Wright, Alison Skinner
2nd row: Kenneth Boyd, Mary Skinner, Margie Wright, Imogene Tift, Norma Boyd, (Bob Storms?), Earl Derwin, Beulah Wright, Connie Thompson
Back row: Mrs. Anderson, Ron Shutts, Maxine Tawney, Lawrence Wright, Norma Mosher, Richard Mosher, Geraldine Boyd, unknown, Norman Wright

Oak Grove 1938 Class - Teacher Abigail Nelson
Front row: Vernon Wright, Doris Boyd, Allison Skinner, Ila Mae Holmes, Harry Wright, Jim Wright, Elaine Derwin, Margaret Shutts, Luella Shutts, Louis Derwin
2nd row: Shirley Tawney, Mary Ann Brock, Marjory Wright, Jim Storms, Mary Skinner, Iris Tift, Beulah Wright, Earl Derwin, Norman Wright, Bob Neilson
3rd row: Harold Wright, Kenneth Boyd
Back row: ? Werts, ? Werts, Connie Thompson, Imogene Tift, Geraldine Boyd, Norma Mosher

The following references are from the journal entries of G. E. G. Wonch, farmer, who lived in the Oak Grove community from 1858 to 1878. He was active with civic duties and one was giving care to the Oak Grove School or District #3 School.

The first school was a log construction. In 1859 the school had five library books which were the most that any of the six schools in the township had at that time. Three of the schools had no library books at all. They spent $2.50 for school repairs that year. A new school at Oak Grove began on Monday, May the 13th, 1867, and Ellen Barton, the Honorable Judge Barton's daughter from Big Prairie, was the teacher. The school was also used for evening singing sessions in the 1860's and 70's. Other functions of the building were as church functions and as a court for the area crimes. In April of 1968 G. E. G. Wonch was appointed as School Board Supervisor for Oak Grove school. On April 20, 1868, Mr. Wonch as School Director, hired Miss Givings to teach the school for 16 weeks at $4 per week and to commence next Monday.

Wonch hired a schoolteacher, Mrs. Meade to whom was to be $5 per week for the school session beginning December 14, 1868. In April, 1869 the school began for a new term of 16 weeks and Ellen Barton was the teacher. Ellen Barton would eventually marry Lewis Stinson and she was born in 1847 and died in 1874. Wonch hired Miss Matilda Smith to teach a new term beginning December 13, 1869. Wonch's next important project of civic business was to find a site for a new school at Oak Grove. They wanted a site on Peter Hall's farm but Hall wanted $75 for the land. School was out on Friday, March 4, 1870 and there was an exhibition in the evening to celebrate the end of the term.

On May 2, 1870 the school began and Miss Mary J. Segar of Newaygo was the teacher. In November of 1870 a school site was purchased from Peter Hall for $50 and a deed was obtained. By autumn in 1871, Wonch was busy on the school specifications and the school board decided to let the job to Nelson Higbee at $1,080 to be completed by the 1st of December, 1871. This was decided on October 5 which allowed less than two months for completion. In November 1871, Wonch did something most every day regarding the schoolhouse until December 9. He began by getting a crank made for the schoolhouse bell, and got a pail, cup and bell rope. He bought $5 worth of stovepipe for the stove they had bought previously. He and Lewis E. Wright hung the bell and put up the stove and pipe. At the start of December, Mr. Wonch and his son Franklin went shopping and bought a chair, doorknobs and a wardrobe for new school. The next day they went to the schoolhouse and put the knobs on the cupboard. He built a fire in the stove to dry the paint and made a key for the front door. In a day or so he blackened the stove and put up wardrobe hooks and drew a supply of wood. On the afternoon of December 9th, they had a dedication of the school W. D. Fuller, Professor Downie and Elder Redcoff were there as speakers. The next day which was Sunday, the area held the first religious meeting in the schoolhouse. Elder Redcoff preached.

In 1874, Wonch had hired Sarah Longcore to teach school at $28 a month. By 1874, the Grange was using the school as a meeting place. In August of 1875, he posted notices of the Compulsory School Law. This law was adopted by the State of Michigan in 1871 establishing the school age from 6 to 16 years. In March of 1875, Wonch hired Miss Ella Meeker to teach an 8 week term of school for $6 per week.

In December of 1875, Lewis Wright was hired as the school teacher at $7 per week.

This Oak Grove class photo was taken in the spring of 1913.
The school burned down in 1914.

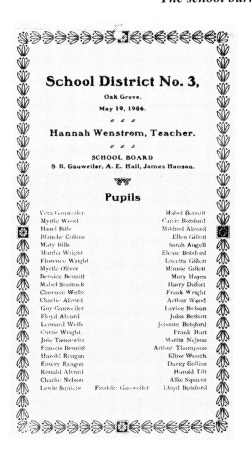

School District No. 3,

Oak Grove.

May 19, 1906.

Hannah Wenstrom, Teacher.

SCHOOL BOARD
S. B. Gauweiler, A. E. Hall, James Hanson.

Pupils

Vera Gauweiler	Mabel Bennitt
Myrtle Wood	Carrie Botsford
Hazel Bills	Mildred Alvord
Blanche Collins	Ellen Gillett
Mary Bills	Sarah Angell
Martha Wright	Eleaze Botsford
Florence Wright	Lowetta Gillett
Myrtle Oliver	Minnie Gillett
Bernice Bennitt	Mary Hayes
Mabel Shattuck	Harry Dufort
Clarence Wells	Frank Wright
Charlie Alvord	Arthur Wood
Guy Gauweiler	Lavine Nelson
Floyd Alvord	John Bennitt
Leonard Wells	Jerome Botsford
Curtis Wright	Frank Hart
Joie Tarnowitz	Martin Nelson
Francis Bennitt	Arthur Thompson
Harold Reagan	Kline Wooch
Emery Reagan	Davey Collins
Ronald Alvord	Harold Tift
Charlie Nelson	Allie Squiers
Lewie Squiers Freddie Gauweiler	Lloyd Botsford

PUPILS

Alfred Alford	Gerold Arthur
Marie Baldwin	Evah Baldwin
James Baldwin	Irwin Baldwin
Jerome Botsford	Lloyd Botsford
Charley Botsford	Russel Canning
Clarence Canning	Lizzie Canning
Davie Collins	Glen Daucer
Marie Dancer	Clara Dunworth
Niel Dunworth	Gerald Dunworth
Freddie Gauwieler	William Hartzell
Glen Hartzell	Gervese Hefferon
Milbern Hefferon	Dorothy Jenkinson
Anna Lentz	Robert Lentz
Fae Lentz	Archie Lowden
Ralph Lowden	Leslie Lowden
Nellie Lowden	Charlie Nelson
Myrtle Oliver	Clarence Overley
Arthur Overley	Vernie Overley
Carl Overley	Ethel Parker
Evelyn Parker	Georgia Shaul
Herman Shaul	Forrest Shutts
Flossie Shutts	Charlie Stray
Francis Thompson	Harold Thompson
Herold Tift	Charlie Wright
Joyce Wright	Clarence Wright
Rachel Wright	Rupert Wright
Zelma Wright	

Teacher Elizabeth Leonard

Olive M. Forwood was born on February 4, 1891. She was 19 years old when she taught one term at Oak Grove School in Croton Township (1909-1910). She taught over 30 children from primary school to high school. The children worked together helping each with the older ones helping younger ones to learn. They were attentive to the lessons, enchanted by the new world their education was opening up to them. Olive may have had her hands full at times with disciplinary problems, but probably not very often. Teachers back then received a great deal of support from parents and children at that time were taught to be more settled. Olive Forwood's teaching career was very short lived. She died unexpectedly of appendicitis on September 30, 1910.

The decorative style of the above picture frames appear to be cloth tied together at the corners giving the appearance of bows. Beside Miss Forwood is an ornately designed wood stove. Everyone wore clothing covering from their necks to their toes. The boys haircuts were typically boyish short around the sides and back. The girls hair styles were pulled away from their faces in pony or pig tails, or short curly styles combed back away from their faces. The facial expressions are ones of wonder, anticipation, antsiness, and "when will this be over." Photography in that time required a number of minutes for the camera to snap the shot.

What wonders school life was then. Chores of the farm and other structured home life were interrupted for school. Some men didn't always like that their boys participated in getting an education instead of helping on the farm during day light hours. But most were proud to have the advancement of education for their children which opened up new life styles and an easier way of life.

Oak Grove High Room - 1923
Ruth Stray is the first girl on the left

Oak Grove School class which included Louise E. (Hall) Grannis

Oak Grove School 1932 class which included Louise E. (Hall) Grannis
Teachers are Clair Dunworth and Mildred Dodge

Oak Grove School 1935 class
Louise E. (Hall) Grannis was 9 years old and a 4th grader.
She is in the center row, fifth from the right

Oak Grove School Student Photos
Late 1950's to Early 1960's

Unidentified students from late 1950's to early 1960's

Gary Rank   *Carol Reid*   *? Wright*   *Rhonda ?*

? Toth   *? Toth*   *? Toth*

Four of Chuck Thomas' school pictures

Four of Billy Westgate's school pictures

Three of Mariann Essenberg's school pictures

Teacher Joy Brisbin 1959-1960

 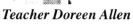  

Teacher Doreen Allen

Rhonda Allen

Teacher Jean Bergman

Three of Robin Thomas' school pictures   *Sharon Emery*

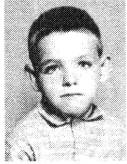  

Three of Kirby Westgate's school pictures   *Laurie Middleton*

Three of Norris Wright's school pictures   *Linda Quick*

Two pictures of Alvin Wright   *Two pictures of Clida Wright*

Pine Grove School

Pine Grove School
School District #5

Pine Grove School was located in Section 26 at the corner of 88th and Beecher Streets. The school annexed to Howard City in 1946.

June 20, 1895 - Newaygo Republican - "School District 5, Croton Township, report for term ending June 7. 19 students enrolled. Not absent during the term: Albert Moore, Frank Peterson, Willie Bowen, Frankie Bowen, John Young, Della Young, Marjory Peterson, Pearl Griffis. Zadie M. Hunter, Teacher

In 1901 the residents of Pine Grove organized a Sunday School to be held at the school.

April 25, 1901 - Newaygo Republican – "Pine Grove School reshingled their roof and Sunday School is held there with a large attendance."

Teachers: Bertha Sahlin, Zadie Hunter

Snowtown School

Elon Howe, who has walked and searched the old logging areas, tells that in the early logging days, Croton Township had three schools located in sections 3 and 4 that were all referred to at one time or another as Snowtown School.

The 1880 plat map shows a school district no. 2 located in Sec. 4 on 52nd Street near the Culp/Snow Log Dam on the Muskegon River.

The second school was located in Sec. 3 on Cypress about a quarter mile south of 48th Street near John F. Snow's Brick Hotel and store.

On the 1922 plat map, the third school is shown located at 52nd and Cypress in Sec. 3.

After the end of the logging era (1854 to early 1900's), the small settlement of Snowtown disappeared from the maps. It is believed that Snowtown school closed sometime in the 1920's.

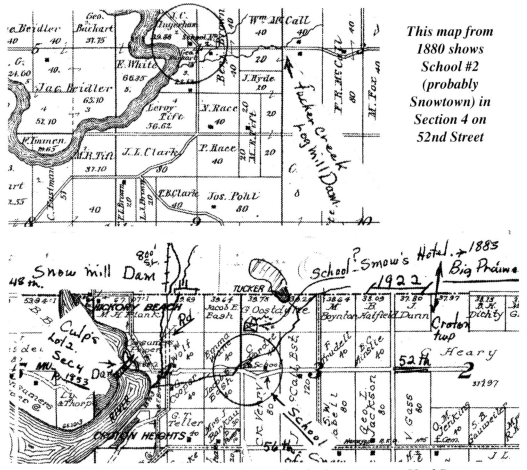

This map from 1880 shows School #2 (probably Snowtown) in Section 4 on 52nd Street

The 1922 map shows a school, believed to be Snowtown on 52nd Street in Section 3 (in circle). Just above the circle may have been the sight of a previous Snowtown school held at Snow's Hotel in 1883.

Ensley Township

   Ensley Township was established in 1858 by taking the six mile square area in the southeastern part of the county away from Croton Township. It is designated as Township 11 North, Range 11 West.

1900

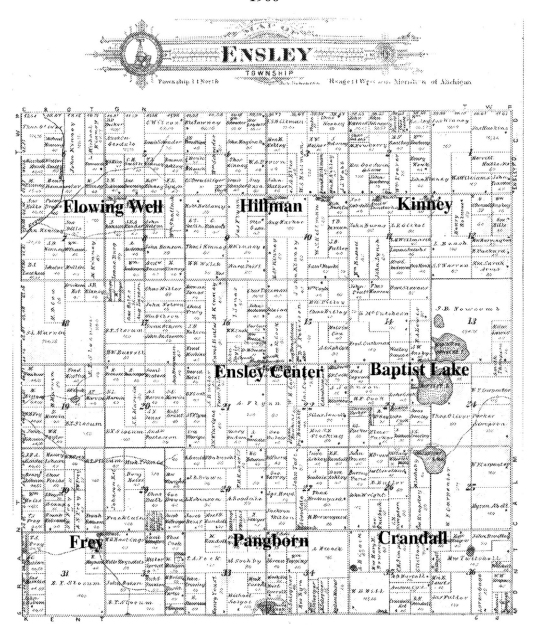

1922

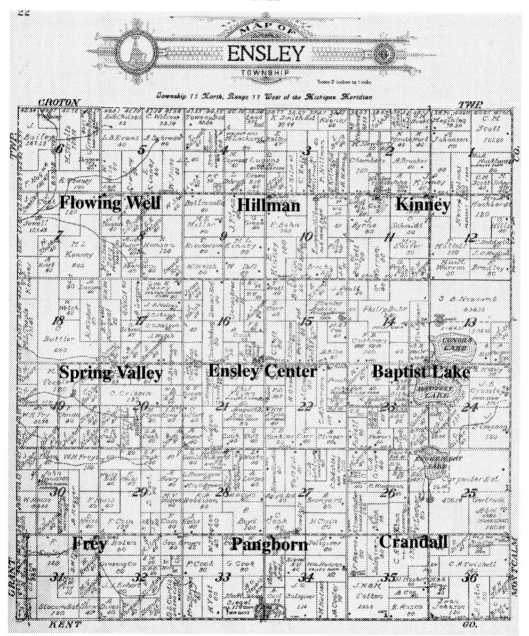

Ensley Township Schools

Ensley Township pioneer Smith Cook established and taught the first school in Ensley Township. Though he did not have proper teacher credentials, he believed that according to Michigan law, he had the qualifications to begin a school. His pupils included his sons, Thomas and James, his brother-in-law, Andrew Flynn, and a fugitive slave named William Bruce, and a few other adults.

Miss Probasco was the first qualified teacher in the township and classes were conducted from her home. Esther Chalk is also mentioned as a teacher who taught out of her home before a schoolhouse was built. It is not known exactly when and where the first schoolhouse was built. There is reference made that it was called Scab school, named after the teacher, Mr. Scab, and located somewhere on Locust Avenue between 104th and 136th Streets.

One record says that the first known schoolhouse was built one mile north of Ensley Center and that a second school was built a one and a quarter mile south of Ensley Center. These schools were discontinued when the school districts were established and new schools built. But, according to published memories of James Kinney of the early days of Ensley, the first schoolhouse in the township was built in the fall of 1859 at the corners one mile south of Ensley Center.

In 1859 there were two school districts. District No. 1 (Hillman School) was located in Section 9 on the northwest corner of 112th Street and Cypress. District No. 2 (Frey School) was located in Section 31 on the southwest corner of 136th Street and Locust. As the population increased, a third school district was organized in 1861 with the school located in Section 35 on the southwest corner of 136th Street and Beech. That school was closed and re-opened as Crandall School in 1868.

There is also a record of tragedy in 1859 when Enos Merritt murdered a young school teacher in Ensley. The reason for this tragedy is not known.

In 1883, there were 363 children attending school with 8 whole school districts and 1 fractional school district. There were 2 male teachers and 16 female teachers employed during the year with the men being paid a total of $240 and the women a total of $1,684.40. That averages out to the men being paid $120 each and the women $105 each.

Schools were added as the population grew and by 1883 there were 8 school districts and 1 fractional school district in the township with the 8 schools being frame built. The school districts were Hillman (#1), Frey (#2), Crandall (#3), Pangborn (#4), Ensley Center (#5) and three others that were later discontinued and replaced (circa early 1900s) by four schools (Flowing Well, Spring Valley, Baptist Lake and Kinney), making a total of nine school districts.

The teachers usually arrived early in the morning during the colder months to start a fire in the woodstove. The children would play games until the school warmed up.

Each school was cleaned each Fall before school began and again in Spring at the end of the school year. The floors were oiled, brush cleaned up, walls cleaned and repairs made.

Each School District owned the approximately one-half acre of land for the school and schoolyard. The land was sold when the schools closed.

Early teacher examinations were given by Cyrus Alton or Theodore S. Frey.

School Inspectors in the 1860 and 1870's were Smith Cook, J.B. Brimley, John Sked,

James Fuller, John Crandall, Andrew Flynn, T.S. Frey, Eugene Hillman, D. McQuarrie, John Taft, George McCutcheon, J.H. Haskin

In 1921 Ensley Township residents voted to form a Rural Agricultural School District, but in 1922 the residents voted down the proposal to build a central high school. So instead of consolidating the schools into one large school, they kept the nine separate schools and administered them all by one school board. Loren Frey said he thought it was the only Rural Agricultural School District to be operated this way.

Prior to the school consolidation, Newaygo, Grant, Howard City and Sand Lake buses would travel the same roads. In 1965, most of the other Newaygo County country schools consolidated into public schools. Ensley Township country school students were initially to integrate with Grant Public Schools. Ensley Township residents were not satisfied with this decision as Howard City and Tri-County schools were a lot closer than Grant. After a year of discussion, a plan was devised that satisfied the majority with Cypress Street being used as the line split to determine which school students would attend – Grant, Howard City or Tri-County. Some in the lower east part of Ensley Township may also have went to Cedar Springs.

Each school had its own bookcase of books for students to use. Upon consolidation of the schools in 1966, the books from all the schools were left at a branch library at Ensley Center where students could continue to use them.

Teachers that taught during the 1860's included Lodeska Clark, Mary Jewell, Parker Simpson, Sarah Baird, Filena Jourdan, A.E. Lounderman, Alma Tibitts, Martha Richmond, C.C. Tibitts, Angelia Gould, S.B. Hoffman, Miss Hill, Emma Jewell, Agnes Jourdan, Miss Whitney, Catherine Givens, Mary Stodard, Hester Richmond, Sarah Sked.

In the 1920's, Ensley township teachers included: Francis Flynn, Janice Berendreght, Bessie Lapree, Emma Abrahamson, Janet Berendreght, Neil Dunworth, Evelyn Williams, Henriette Zank (her son, Carl later became treasurer of one of the schools), Marie Toft, Veda Elinard, Ethel Galster, Mabel Gibson, Marie Mansfield, Bryant Williams, Earl Galster, Marie Dunworth, Reathel Dodge, Delila Boyd, Luella Kirchmeyer, Leila Starn, Elsie Gibson, Norma Preston.

Ensley Township teachers in the 1930's included: Virginia Johnson, Nora Mast, Donald Jeffers, Kenneth Albrecht, Jennie Diekema, Norma Preston, Evelyn Brown, May Robinson, Ida Smith, Gertrude Simcox, Bessie LaPreze, Helen Dunworth, Anne Hefferan, Marie Dunworth, Lorene Hoag, Maurice Cochrane, Robert Merlington, Madeleine Hefferan, Ronald Benton, Delila Gorby, Leona Dodge, Eloise (Carlson) Norquist, Margaret McCallum, Lucile Brydges, Alice Swanson, Wealtha Barbour, Lucile Raines.

In the 1920's, the teacher's monthly pay ranged from $80 to $105 depending on the number of students. During the Depression in the 1930's, the teacher's pay dropped to a total $25-70 per month, but because of a shortage of funds, the teachers were paid half a month's salary and later paid the remaining amount when funds were available. By the 1950's, the pay was up to $4,200 for the year.

Aug. 21, 1941 Newaygo Republican – "Teachers this 1941 school year for Ensley Township: Ronald Benton (Ensley Center), Grey Regan (Frey), James Herin (Pangborn), Bessie LaPreze (Crandell), Gretchen, Isabell and Beatrice Bryant (Kinney, Flowing Well and Hillman). Crystal Race will be in charge of music this year."

In the 1940's, the 8th grade graduation ceremonies for the township were held in Sand Lake.

March 14, 1940 - Newaygo Republican

Ensley School history told

Consolidation Has Made Possible Many Economies in System

The following account, written by a trustee of the Ensley consolidated school board gives a brief account of the development of the school system in that district:

"Our nine Ensley schools were each a separate unit, operated independently, under guidance of a board of three trustees, until seventeen years ago last July. The teacher was hired for one to three months, and if satisfactory, the contract was renewed for another term. Some schools were very large in winter when the young men attended and it was government, force of character, or even might that counted much.

"In an early day, when the saw mills were running, as many as seventy pupils are reported attending in a not too large schoolhouse. The seats were long benches, fastened to the wall on three sides of the room, and there were no desks in which to keep books. The small children swung their feet, as many could not reach the floor. The larger boys, some of them grown men, would go until they got through their books, especially arithmetic.

"It was not until about 1899 that a class completed the eighth grade in Ensley and graduation exercises were held.

"About this time the teachers were paid around thirty dollars per month in winter and a little less in the spring and fall, and a few of the schools had enrollments of fifty. But with pupils graduating, enrollments declined until the smaller schools had only six to eleven pupils and the largest about forty. Teachers wages climbed and requirements were raised. In the old days a third grade certificate was needed and if the candidate failed to pass and still had a school to teach, the county commissioner would issue a special certificate good untill the next examination. During the 1920's teachers were paid from $65 to $100 per month.

"Each district voted a different rate of tax; buildings could not be kept up; the book question was serious when families had to move to another district. In July, 1922, on petition by the late Isaac Hawkins, and a helper to the township, a motion was carried that a new school be built according to state specifications but the motion to bond was voted down so the school was never built. We operate, however, with five trustees acting as a board of education.

"Taxes were equalized, teachers wages are as high as when we were voting three times as much money; we find it easier, since consolidating, to repair buildings, care for grounds, and bring equipment to standard. Our lighting system, through much improved, is still in the making. We have been in a position to receive government help and now hire a full-time music and handicraft teacher.

"About twenty pupils finish our schools each year and we have no building large enough to house the throng that comes to our exercises. This year we are transporting 60 pupils to high school. Each year about 40 evergreen trees are set out and it is hoped that this practice will be continued by the generations to follow."

Edna Swanson Heiss memories

Edna Swanson and her family moved to Ensley Township when she was about 18 months old. She attended Frey School and graduated from Grant High School in 1929. She remembered that because her family lived so far from the high school, she and her siblings would go to town on Sunday night or early Monday morning during the winter months and stay with another family for the school week, returning home for the week-end.

Edna attended Western Michigan College to earn a teaching degree. She returned to Western Michigan University in 1966 to earn her Bachelor of Science degree in teaching. Edna taught kindergarten through eighth grade in a one-room schoolhouse in Grant until 1937.

Edna married Theodore (Ted) Heiss and they had three children. They eventually settled in Ensley Township in 1946. Edna had many offers to go back to teaching but she refused until she found someone to take care of her young children. She started teaching sixth grade in Grant. She found that teaching a class of 40 sixth graders was quite a bit different than teaching in a one-room country school. After a couple of years, she went back to teaching in a country school where the total number of students ranged from 20 to 30 students. She found that in the country school setting, students were more likely to help out and showed respect for their school.

Edna taught in several country schools including Birch School in Kent County, Rice Lake in Grant Township, Pangborn, Crandall, Kinney and Ensley Center schools in Ensley Township. By now, though, country schools began consolidating into the larger school districts. Edna accepted a position teaching first grade at Grant Elementary School, which she found suitable for her. She continued teaching first grade until she retired in 1975.

There had been many changes taking place in education in the 1970's and Edna expressed her feelings in a 1996 interview:

"The one that really stands out in this day is the changes in discipline. At that time you could punish a youngster for doing something wrong, but now that is not allowed. A lot of this stems from a lack of discipline in the family. There is a real lack of discipline in the family now, with children not having enough responsibility. We had much responsibility with the chores we had at home, and also with having to walk to and from school everyday.

"There is also quite a difference in subject matter. We had to learn what we were being taught in school; we didn't have computers or calculators then. Dates seemed to be more important also. Places and dates are no longer important to education anymore. Reading and learning of poetry was also stressed.

"I feel that consolidation was a mistake. The rural students were doing so well. We had a different type of teaching in the country schools. Children worked much harder and developed better study skills. In country schools, the older students would help the younger students with their lessons. It also seems that students have lost respect for their teachers, elders, parents, and even their own personal property. Children don't respect things that they own anymore."

Note: John Swanson, father of Edna and Alice Swanson, served as township school treasurer for many years.

June, 1894 Newaygo Republican

Six schools in the Grove area in Ensley Township had a picnic. The following teachers were present: District #2 Maggie Fortune, #3 Florence Rush, #5 May Phoenix and Rena Baker, #8 Bessie Hall, #9 Lottie Fisk.

Ensley Township
1917 Commencement Program

Ensley Township Union Commencement Exercises

Tuesday evening, June Twelfth
nineteen hundred seventeen
Eight o'clock

Baptist Church

Ensley Center

✕✕✕✕

Baccalaureate Sermon, Sunday evening
7:30, June 10, by Rev. Merriman.

✕✕✕✕

Motto: Onward and Upward.
Colors: Green and White.
Flower: White Carnation.

Program

March	
Invocation	Rev. Merriman
Solo "My Task"	Mrs. Eugene Hillman
Address	Dr. Deal, Lansing
Quartette	"Shadows of Twilight"
Class Song	
Presentation of Diplomas	

✕✕✕✕

Teachers

District No. 1. Mrs. Alfred Johnson
District No. 2. Blanche Welch
District No. 3. Ray Rollison
District No. 4. Mr. Branyon
District No. 5. Stacia Donahue
District No. 6. Gertrude Vander Molen
District No. 7. Gladys Douglas
District No. 9. Byron Place

Graduates

District No. 1
 Hazel Hackbardt
 Lysle Holmes
 Florence Cain
 Bertha Bradley

District No. 2
 Glowina Denton
 Roy Keeney

District No. 3
 Elma Topping

District No. 4
 Walter Winters
 Richard Blackburn

District No. 5
 Nida Cook
 Florence Carr
 Emma Abrahamson
 Herschel Beebe

District No. 6
 Robert Simcox

District No. 7
 Clayton Simpson
 Lucy Patin

District No. 9
 Walter Swanson
 Charles Cook

Baptist Lake School

Baptist Lake School
School District No. 6

Baptist Lake was named after the lake that is was near. It was located in Section 14 on 120th Street just east of Butternut Street. The school got its name from the lake it was located nearby.

The school closed between the years of 1941 and 1945 due to low enrollment but was reopened in 1946 when the student population increased.

Teachers: Rena Becker (1895), Sadie Kinney (circa 1906), Mable Kinney (1919), Jeanette Roberts (1959)

1919 graduate: John Simcoe

Baptist Lake School Class circa 1946
Front row: Margaret Simcoe, Wesley Simcoe, Janet Bergman, Dorothy Beach,
    Tom Paulson
2nd row: Bill Bergman, Kenneth Cook, Leon Oakes, Ella Donna Hyrns,
    Ruth Bowers, Shirley Oakes
3rd row: David Bergman, Raymond Cook, Gary Albrecht, Dale Paulson, Alva Hyrns,
    Leon Tawney, Theodore Beach
4th row: Viola Bowers, Evelyn Woodman, Marilyn Bergman. Teacher is Maxine
    Muehlhauser

Crandall School

Crandall School
School District No. 3

The school was named after the John Crandall Family who settled in Ensley Township in 1856. The school was located in Section 35 at the corner of 136th Street and Beech.

John Crandall married Mary Clawson and they had two children, Eugene and Ida. John served as school director for 16 years.

In November 1901, the school closed for several weeks due to an outbreak of diptheria. The teacher, Miss Maud Maynard, returned to her home in the village of Newaygo until school resumed.

Teachers: Ann McCutcheon (1887), Florence Rush (1894), Maud Maynard (1901), Ray Rollison (1917), Ida Woods (1919), Gertrude Simcoe (1959)

Graduates: 1917 - Elma Topping; 1919 - Aloysius Patin and Lionel Cox

Excerpts from the Cedar Springs Democrat:

Feb. 2, 1887 – "Ann McCutcheon is giving good satisfaction teaching the Crandall school we hear. We always thought she would."

Feb. 10, 1887 – "There is some talk of having preaching at the Crandall school house again; hope so."

Crandall School

Crandall School Class circa 1910
Seated: Clayton Simpson, Esther Strayer, Lottie Bradley, Lucy Patin, Roma
*   Strowbridge, Ivah Bradley, Marie Blood*
Center row: Teacher Hilda Johnson and Josie Moore
Back row: August Patin, Bessie Strayer, Bertha Hartle, Ruth Simpson, Nellie Moore,
*   Walter Moore, Shirley Hartle, Inda Powers, Maude Blood, Gurner Salsgiver,*
*   Lennie Grove, Phillip Patin*

Ensley Center School

Ensley Center School
School District No. 5

Ensley Center School was located in Section 16 at the corner of 120th Street and Cypress. It was named due to it being located near the center of the township.

The original school was replaced by a cement block building in the early 1900's. The building now serves as the Township Hall.

Teachers: May Phoenix (1894), Rena Baker (1894), Stacia Donahue (1917), Evelyn Williams (1919), Ronald Benton, Eloise Norquist (1951-1953), Edna Heiss (1959), Mr. Brooks

1917 graduates: Nida Cook, Florence Carr, Emma Abrahamson, Herschel Beebe
1919 graduates: Carlton Beitner, Wayne Cook and Arnold Carr

Dan Graham's memories:

In 1963, two boys from Hillman were sent to Ensley Center School. These two boys, Ken and Paul, received excessive disciplinarian treatment by the teacher. He had Paul hold books in hands extended from body to full length, if Paul dropped a little the teacher used a wooden ruler to hit Paul's hands on the backside of his hands, all this in front of K-8th grade students. I told my father and mother what happened. They went to the school board along with several other parents and filed a complaint which resulted in the teacher's termination.

I remember in November 1963 we found out that President Kennedy had been shot in Texas and later we were told he died. I think that was the saddest day I ever had in school. I was the aide that day answering or helping any younger students who raised his or her hand.

Softball was one of the more popular sports and all teams were not only coed but also multi-graded. Another popular sport was Red Rover or Annie Eye Over.

At the end of the 8th grade all township 8th graders came to the Ensley Center School for a test to see at what grade level you were capable of and the highest score would be the class valedictorian and the second highest the salutatorian. I was valedictorian and had to give a speech in the auditorium in Croton to over 300 people. I couldn't give an oral report in high school afterwards.

When I was in kindergarten, 1955, I ran in the school and teacher Eloise Norquist took me by my ear and walked me around the classroom all the time explaining why we do not run in school.

One year we were told that a former student Oliver Cotton, who had enlisted and was sent to Viet Nam, had fallen under fire. He had two younger siblings in the school, Dennis and Debra.

1956-1961 which were 1st through 6th grade, our teacher was Mrs. Edna Heiss. She was a good teacher and a fair and just disciplinarian.

Two nuns would come to the school usually fall or spring and give free vaccinations to all the students.

In 2nd or 3rd grade I was pushed off the top of the slide and my chest hit the support pipe on the way down and I had the breath knocked out of me for about two minutes.

In 3rd grade during the winter I walked home, which started sunny and warm, throwing snowballs with which caused my gloves to get wet. About three-quarters of a mile home a storm came in and I got frost bite on my hands and feet and my sinuses were messed up.

My teachers were: Kindergarten Mrs. Norquist, 1st through 6th Mrs. Heiss, and 7th and 8th Mr. Brooks.

Ensley Center Class
Front row: Millard Cook, Earl Hudson, Lymon Flynn, Glen Gillett, John Flynn, Floyd Knox, Everett List.

2nd row: Jennie Butler, Mable Flynn, Erma Knox, Nida Cook, Esther Anderson, Hazel Flynn (behind Esther), Florence Carr, Mary Flynn, Emma Abrahamson, Meda Abrahamson.

3rd row: Ida Carr, Sadie Jones, Oscar Green, Ernest Abrahamson, Kenneth Hahn (behind Ernest), Effie Kinney

4th row: Bertha Jewell, Anna Hawkins, Lyle Flynn, Myrtle Carr, Hazel Green, Paul Anderson, Illian Olson, William Abrahamson, Teacher Sadie Kinney

Ensley Center School 1900 Class
Front row: ? Fallman, Ed Hawkins, Ernest Hawkins, Leonard Butler, Herman Anderson, Leon Jewell, Don Cook, Nora Cook, Gladys Dancer, Mabel Cook?, Maudie Harper, Hazel Stilwill, Mabel Kinney.
Back row: Cleve Cook, Lee Butler, Phil Flynn, Fred Fallman?, Alta Hammer, Della Youngs, Addie Jones, Helen Cook, preacher's daughter, Teacher J.C. Kritzer, Daisy Jones, Eunice Fallman, Mary Hawkins, Amy Olson, Helen Farrell.

Ensley Center School 1927 Class
Front row: Paul Mosher, Ralph Jones, Bernie Olson, Robert Jones
2nd row: Robert Loft, Martin VanIddeking, Truman Cochrane, Allen Cook, Donald
*   Jones, Clayton Cook, Vern Carr*
3rd row: Melba Jones, Crystal Denton (visiting), Donna Cook, Donna Bitner,
*   Jane DeBlaay, Francis Richards, Mary DeBlaay, Edna Flynn*
4th row, Leona Flynn, Irene Flynn, Helen Welch, Lola Bitner, Violet Carr, Lucy
*   Jones, Frances Jones, Dorothy Pratt, Mary Pratt, Viola Flynn,*
*   Jessie VanIddeking.*
5th row: Dan Peterson, Martin VanIddeking, Archie Carr, Teacher Neil Dunworth,
*   Roger DeBlaay, Howard Cook, Elton Cook*

Ensley Center School 1946 Class
Front row: Bill Cook (3rd boy), Philip Hanes (5th boy), Ruth Hanes (9th girl),
*   Jack Flynn (11th boy), John Flynn (12th boy)*
2nd row: Joan Flynn (4th girl), Bob Flynn (7th boy), Jeanette Roberts (8th girl),
*   Linda Hanes (9th girl)*
3rd row: Audrey Cook (2nd girl), Shirley McTavish (3rd girl), Nora Cook (4th girl)
4th row: Thomas (Bud) Graham, Teacher Nadine Cook (third), Rachel Crispin,
*   Ruth Crispin (5th girl)*

Ensley Center School Students 1956-57

JoAnn Baker	Joyce Baker	Cheryl Beutner	Larry Brugel	Genevive Carr
Ollie Cotten	Mark DeJong	Sharon DeJong	Dick Hanes	Karl Hanes
Marcella Hanes	Phyllis Hanes	Garth Keisler	Judy MacTavish	Sandra MacTavish
Jerry Roberts	Joyce Roberts	Frances Uhe	Marie Uhe	Unknown

Mrs. Edna Heiss
Teacher 1956-57

Ensley Center School Students 1957-1960

JoAnn Baker
1957-58

Joyce Baker
1957-58

Samuel Cook
1957-58

Mark DeJong
1957-58

Michael Graham
1957-58

Dick Hanes
1957-58

Phyllis Hanes
1957-58

Sandra MacTavish
1957-58

Joyce Roberts
1957-58

Margaret Uhe
1957-58

Denny Cotten
1959-60

Dick Hanes
1959-60

Marcella Hanes
1959-1960

Max Hanes
1959-1960

Phyllis Hanes
1955-56

Joyce Roberts
1958-59

Ensley Center School Students

Dick Hanes

Karl Hanes

Philip Hanes

Phyllis Hanes provided the class photos of Ensley Center students.

Marcella Hanes

Marcella Hanes

Phyllis Hanes

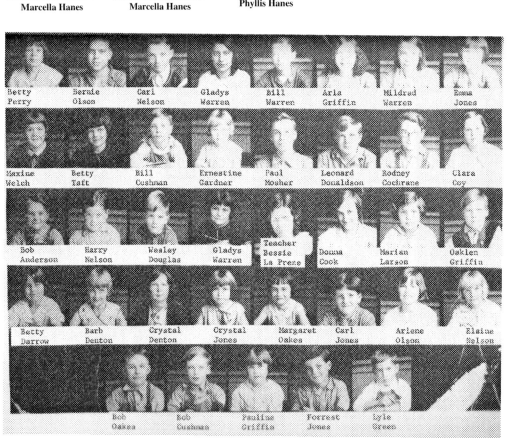

Betty Perry	Bernie Olson	Carl Nelson	Gladys Warren	Bill Warren	Arla Griffin	Mildred Warren	Emma Jones
Maxine Welch	Betty Taft	Bill Cushman	Ernestine Gardner	Paul Mosher	Leonard Donaldson	Rodney Cochrane	Clara Coy
Bob Anderson	Harry Nelson	Wesley Douglas	Gladys Warren	Teacher Bessie La Prese	Donna Cook	Marian Larsen	Oaklen Griffin
Betty Darrow	Barb Denton	Crystal Denton	Crystal Jones	Margaret Oakes	Carl Jones	Arlene Olson	Elaine Nelson
Bob Oakes	Bob Cushman	Pauline Griffin	Forrest Jones	Lyle Green			

Ensley Center School 1930-31

Ensley Center School 1960 Class
Front row: Jay Harrison, Martha Uhe, Robert McTavish, James Uhe
2nd row: Robert Ellick, Roger Carr, Ollie Cotten, Thomas Graham,
*   Judy McTavish, Cindy Pratt, Debbie Coten*
3rd row: Margaret Uhe, JoAnne Baker, Mark DeJong, Maurice Carr,
*   Max Hanes, Donald Pratt*
4th row: Teacher Edna Heiss, Joyce Baker, Marcella Hanes, Gary
*   DeJong, Ronald Cook, Patricia Cochrane, Frances Uhe*
5th row: Larry Cook, Michael Graham, Carl Hanes, Genevieve Carr,
*   Marie Uhe*

Flowing Well School

Flowing Well School
School District No. 10

In August 1881, Benjamin Ogden leased a portion of land in Sec. 8 to the School District for $26. The land was leased to the school district for as long as there was a school there with the condition that the school district would build and keep in repair a tight board fence on the east and south sides of the school. The school was located at the corner of 112th Street and Locust and named for the many artesian wells or springs in the area.

After 1885, Catherine Mabee, Charles Rood and Frank Topping owned and continued to lease the land to the school district. In 1938 Mary Topping gave a warranty deed to the school district for $1. A new brick school was built circa 1907 with the old structure being sold to John and Minnie (Topping) Butler and moved one-quarter mile west and used as their residence.

Teachers: Cleo Symons (1919), Mrs. Cramer (1959). Matie Warren taught for two years at Flowing Well, left the area and then returned to Ensley to marry. She boarded with the Hanson family and later married Nels Hanson. She is credited with starting the Patron's Day observances in Ensley Township schools. (Matie taught circa 1918-1930).

1919 graduate: Bert Alverson

1896-1897 Flowing Well – Teacher was Della M. Grant; Director was Frank Topping; Pupils: Jennie Pettie, Fred Hanson, Nelse Hanson, Blinda Hanson, Ralph Downing, Rosie Downing, Minnie Topping, Frankie Tannewitz, Charlie Tannewitz, Johnnie Hanson, Pearl Pettit, Linnie Topping, Florence Shattuck, Roy Jenkinson, Willie Tannewitz, Inez Shattuck, Ethel Rice, Louis Wilcox, May Wilcox, Charlie Harding, Teressa Petit, Tommy Pettit, Maggie Lynch, Willie Lynch, Arthur Shattuck, Nora Lynch.

Topping Family History

Mary Dodge and her parents came to Newaygo in the early 1880s. In early 1883 she married Frank Topping and they moved to a farm east of Newaygo, in an area later known as the "Little Prairie". Frank and Mary later moved to the "Goyte Farm" in the northwest corner of Ensley Township. Here their children Lena, Elva and Glenn were born. In 1898 they bought 40 acres, minus one half acre for the school house, from the estate of Charles C. Rood. Frank and Mary were active in community affairs and living next to the schoolhouse, the teacher would usually room and board in the Topping home. In later years when the school needed to expand, they donated more land to the school.

John and Minnie Butler were married in 1907. Minnie was a daughter of Frank and Mary Topping. John and Minnie bought land directly west of School District #10, later known as Flowing Well School. They cleared the land. They needed a house to live in and as the School District had decided to build a new school house, they bought the old one. They moved the building about one eighth of a mile west to their farm. In 1913 with the help of friends and neighbors, they had a barn raising. They lived in the school house until 1918 when they built a large field stone home.

Gloria Topping, who gave a warranty deed to the school district for $1 in 1938 is pictured next to the Flowing Well School.

Fountain located on the east side of the Flowing Well Schoolhouse (District No. 3), Ensley Township. This well accounts for the name of the school. The house is the home of Frank Topping, and the corn is part of the Toppings' garden plot. The pine stump was

a part of the landscape for a number of years after the school was built. It may have been there when the second brick building school was constructed. The mailbox indicates that the picture was taken after the formation of R.F.D. delivery service which began circa 1903. The picture was taken by Mrs. Will Patterson (nee Anna Tannewitz) who had a photography business at the Tannewitz' home on Bill's Lake in Croton Township.

Flowing Well School Class Circa 1908

Front row: Sadie Alverson, Laura Shutts, Elva Topping, Ellen Hanson, Ruth Anderson, Johnie Saunders, Etta Shutts, Bertha Squires, Julia Hanson, Alberta Saunders, Ethel Saunders, Blanche Alverson, Delbert

Downing, Glen Topping, Oscar Hanson, George Hanson, Lewis Squires.
  Back row: Emil Hanson, Teacher Katheryn North, Hans Hanson, Eddie Phillips, Harry Cooper, Harry Hanson

Flowing Well School 1925 Classroom
Left row (front to rear): Sidney Cook, Robert Carpenter (Stults), Donald Butler,
*   Laurence Boyd, Foster Butler, Leonard Butler (standing)*
2nd row: Nels Junior Hanson, Clayton Cook, Geore Norwood, Opal Johnson,
*   Nelda Butler*
3rd row: Helen Evans, William Tucker, Margarite Griffes, Sarah Norwood,
*   Norma Butler*
4th row: Verna Cook, Willie Griffes, Francis Porter, Neva Butler
Teacher Marie Dunworth (standing)
Absent from photo: Carl Hanson and Iva Griffes

Frey School

Frey School
School District No. 2

Frey School, named after the T.S. Frey family, was one of the first schools to be built in the township. It was located in Section 31 at the corner of 136th Street and Locust.

Teachers: Anna Marvin taught in the 1880's (she later married S. Wilbur Frey. She was paid $112 for 4 months in 1882. She also taught at Goodwell in 1883 for the 4 month winter term), Maggie Fortune (1894), Blanche Welch (1917), Lavinnie Curtiss (1919), Neil Dunworth (1959), Miss Williams, Mrs. Brown, Delila (Boyd) Gorby, May Robinson Hill, Alice Swanson, Mrs. Jennie Green

1917 graduates: Glowina Denton, Roy Keeney
1919 graduate: Albin Schuitema

Frey School Class Circa 1923-1924
Front row: Robert Fisk, Russel Hoover, Esward Fisk, Lawrence Englert,
Loren Frey, Stanley Dickerson
2nd row: Sybel Cavendar, Marie Robinson, Dorlene Heiss, Vivian Heiss,
Ella Frey, Blanch Dickerson
3rd row: Lester Englert, Lloyd Hoover, Edna Swanson, Teacher Jennie Green,
Laird Hoover, Bob Cavendar, Robert McCluen

Frey School 1925 Class
Front row: Lawrence Englert, Loren Frey, Robert McCluen, Stanley Dickerson
2nd row: Robert Fisk, Edward Fisk, Billy Heiss, Ella Frey, Blanch Dickerson,
? Bradley, Vivah Hoover
3rd row: Russel Hoover, Lloyd Hoover, Teacher Alice Swanson, Lester Englert,
Laird Hoover, Marie Robinson, Sybel Cavendar, Dorlene Heiss, Vivian Heiss

Frey Family History

The Frey School was named after the Theodore S. Frey family. Theodore S. Frey, also known as Elder Frey or T.S. Frey, was a minister who officiated many marriages in his circuit and also held many township positions. (T.S. Frey's great-grandson, Loren Frey still has many of the marriage licenses from those early years in his possession.) T.S. Frey came to Ensley Township in 1867 with his wife, the former Rachel Vail Line. They had three children, Alton, Mary Louise (drowned a few years after arriving in Ensley Township), and S. Wilbur. Alton was educated by his parents at the Frey School. Alton married teacher Dora Watson and they had five children, Dora Althea, Rachel Diantha, Theodore A., Bessie M. and Ada Mae. Dora died after the birth of Ada Mae. Alton re-married several times more and moved west.

S. Wilbur Frey married Anna (Annie) Marvin, a teacher at Frey School. Annie was also a very successful beekeeper in the area. Wilbur and Annie had three children, Harold, Daisy and Harry. Harold married Dora Ella Borten and their two children are Loren and

Ella. Loren Frey still lives on the family farm. Daisy married Glen Cain and Harry married Blanch Verburg.

Neil Dunworth was Loren Frey's teacher when he was a beginner. Mr. Dunworth came back to teach in the 1950's when there was a shortage of teachers. May Robinson was Loren's 8th grade teacher.

The winter of 1936 was an especially snowy year with the snow piling up more than 3 feet, but that didn't stop teacher Ronald Benton who never missed a single day of school that winter. The snow was packed down hard so that cars could drive over the roads.

Loren Frey was elected Treasurer/Secretary in July 1961 and he continued until the schools consolidated in 1966. He replaced Auberg Norquist. Loren still has most of the school records including school board meeting minutes, lists the teachers, their wages, and school finances.

Loren also remembered that in 1966, a milk truck delivered milk to the schools for the students' lunch and that Gertrude Manley cooked lunch for the children for a few years.

Loren donated a 42-star school flag (pictured below) to the Newaygo County Society of History & Genealogy. The flag was never used because the 43rd state was admitted to the United States soon after, making the 42-star flag obsolete.

Public Schools of Michigan.

CONTRACT.

It is hereby contracted and agreed between the District Board of District No. _2_, in the Township of _Easley_, County of _Newaygo_, and State of Michigan, and _Anna Marvin_, a legally qualified teacher in said Township, that the said _Anna Marvin_ shall teach the primary school of said district for the term of _Four_ months, commencing on the _Ninth_ day of _October_, A. D. 188_2_; and the said _Anna Marvin_ agrees faithfully to keep a correct list of pupils, and the age of each attending school, and the number of days each pupil is present, and to furnish the Director of the district with a correct copy of the same at the close of the school, and to observe and enforce the rules and regulations established by the District Board.

The said District Board, in behalf of said district, agrees to keep the school house in good repair, and to provide the necessary fuel, and to pay said _Anna Marvin_ for the said service as teacher, to be faithfully and truly rendered and performed, the sum of _112_ dollars, the same being the amount of wages above agreed upon, to be paid on or before the _9_ day of _February_ 188_3_; Provided, that in case said _Anna Marvin_ shall be dismissed from school by the District Board for gross immorality, or violation of this contract, or shall have _certificate annulled or suspended by the Township Superintendent of Schools, or other lawful authority, shall not be entitled to any compensation from and after such annulment, suspension or dismissal.

In witness whereof, we have hereunto subscribed our names this _26_ day of _Sept_ A. D. 188_2_.

Miller Sprout
O. B. Robinson   District Board.

J. A. P. Mason, Publisher, Centreville, Mich.

Anna Marvin Teacher.

MICHIGAN TEACHERS' INSTITUTES.
Certificate of Membership.

I Hereby Certify, That _____ was a Member of the _____ County Teachers' Institute, held at _____ to _____ 188_, and that __ was in attendance _ half-days, as shown in the following schedule:

WEEKS.	MONDAY.		TUESDAY.		WEDNESDAY.		THURSDAY.		FRIDAY.	
	A. M.	P. M.	A. M.	P. M.	A. M.	P. M.	A. M.	P. M.	A. M.	P. M.
First Week.										
Second Week.										

This certificate is granted in accordance with the provisions of Sec. 4 Act No. 33, Laws of 1877, as amended by Act No. 112, Laws of 1883; and should be recognized by School Officers in the examination and the employment of teachers.

HERSCHEL R. GASS,

YEAR	SOCIAL SECURITY NO.	SEX	NAME
58-59		F	EDNA HEISS

SAND LAKE

DEGREE	MARITAL STATUS	DEP.	LOCAL ADDRESS
	M		

DATE EMPLOYED	DATE LEFT	POSITION	SCHOOL
9-1-58		TEACHER	CENTER

QUARTERLY SUMMARY OF EARNINGS

YEAR	Q	AMT. EARNED	RETIREMENT AND F.I.C.A.		TAX WITHHELD
	1				
	2				
	3	444.43	23.33		41.00
	4				
	1				
	2				

SALARY	ADDITIONS TO REGULAR PAY	ABSENCE NO. OF DAYS	CODE	DEDUCTIONS	GROSS AMOUNT EARNED	RETIREMENT AND F.I.C.A.	TAX WITHHELD	HOSPITALIZATION			NET PAY	PAY PERIOD	CHECK NUMBER	
1											170.06	9-12-58	3949	1
2					444.43	23.33	41.00				380.09	9-23-58	3967	2
3											190.0			3
4					444.45	23.33	41.00				380.12	10-21-58	4018	4
5														5
6					444.45	23.38	41.00				380.12	11-20-58	4044	6
7														7
8					444.45	23.33	41.00				380.12	12-15-58	4072	8
9														9
10					444.45	24.42	41.00				379.03	1-19-59	4114	10
11														11
12					444.45	24.42	41.00				379.03	2-20-59	4150	12
13														13
14					444.45	24.42	41.00				379.03	3-16-59	4188	14
15				4										15
16					444.45	24.42	41.00				379.03	4-13-59	4222	16
17														17
18					444.45	24.42	41.00				379.03	5-13-59	4254	18
19	Teachers Salary			66.66	3.66	6.13					56.87	5-25-59		19
20	Library Pay			66.66	3.66	6.13					56.87	5-25-59		20
21				133.32	7.32	12.30					113.70	5-25-59		21
22														22

SCHOOL INDIVIDUAL PAYROLL RECORD

Edna Heiss' teacher's pay record for the 1958-59 school year.

Hillman School

Hillman School
School District No. 1

Hillman School was located in Section 10 at the corner of 104th Street (also known as Kendaville) and Cypress. In the early years its was part of School District No. 2, but when the school districts were restructured it became School District No. 1. The first Hillman school, which was named after the William S. Hillman family, was built across the street in Section 9 and later was moved to Section 10.

In the school report of Nov. 3, 1887, there were 38 students enrolled with an average attendance of 21.

During the 1940's Rose Peterson provided hot lunches to the school through a government program.

The PTA group held a box social fundraiser to buy a piano for the school for $20. The group also held other school fundraisers selling peanuts and candy (1941 cost: Peanuts – 10# $1.30 1# walnuts $.75; Candy – 10# $1.00; 5# $.50; 2# $.30)

The school oil stove and gas lamps were disposed of in October 1938.

Hillman School students fondly remember the baseball games played against Ensley Center. The kids would pile into the teacher's car, even sitting in the trunk, to travel to the school they competed against two miles down the road.

Loren Frey recalled the story of a deer hunter who shot his rifle near Hillman School property resulting in the bullet entering the school and lodging in the blackboard behind the teacher's desk. Fortunately, no one was hurt.

Hillman consolidated with Tri-County in 1967.

Today (2011), the school building is owned by the Bird family which also owns the Bird's Market across the street from the school.

Teachers: Kittie Backart (1887), Ruth Hall (1895), Mrs. Alfred Johnson (1917), Beatrice Bryant (1940-1942), Nora Mast (1942-1946), Lenora Taft (1946-1947) Eloise Norquist (1947-1950), Rachel Crispin (1958-1959), Jeanette (Roberts) VanderHaag (1959-1960), Jean Bergman (1961)

1887 students: Hazel Nellis, Robert Peterson, Anna Bellamy, Mildred Doyil, Eddie Boughden, Lettie Nellis, John Mathews, Frank Boughden, Elmer Doyil, Sherman Van Liew, Libbie Terwilliger, Eddie Kelley

In 1909-1910, there were three Kinney children in attending Hillman School: Don, Lena and Tom.

1917 graduates: Hazel Hackbardt, Lysle Holmes, Florence Cain, Bertha Bradley

Hillman School 1909-1910 Class

Back row: Raymond Shattuck, John Mathews, Clyde Mathews, Blanche Welch, unknown, Mabel Kinney, Leone Denton, Bertha Geise, John Ellis
Middle row: Gertrude Wood, teacher Mike Denton, Mary Kinney, Helen Geise, Phil Shattuck, Veronica Kinney, Minnie Geise, Ed Lyons, Fannie Flynn, Ruth Jones, Glo Denton, Cecil Brook, Willie Mathews, Don Kinney, George Flynn, Paul Tawney
Front row: Leonard Tawney, Will Shattuck, Thelma Mathews, Lena Kinney, Blanche Bohn, Tom Kinney, Gus Bohn, Delbert Denton

Memories of Dale K. Bellamy

Dale K. Bellamy attended Hillman School from Kindergarten to eighth grade, from 1944 to 1953. Dale is the son of Oliver and Leona Bellamy who lived on Elm Street. Lunchtime typically included a packed lunch of either lunch meat or peanut butter and jelly sandwich, fruit and milk. During recess time, students played softball, anyeye over, mumbley peg, tag, and simon says. Special programs were given during PTA meetings and the annual Christmas party. Dale remembers that the teacher would have the boys bring in wood from the wood shed every morning and fill the woodbox by the furnace. Students would take turns ringing the bell for recess and lunch. Every spring, Hillman School students would play softball against the other schools in the area. Dales' teachers included Miss Nora Mast, Lenora Taft, Eloise Norquist, Ronald Benton, Alice Swanson and Joy Brisbin. Dale's 1951 classmates included Beulah Cooper, Bev, Dale, Gene and Ron Bellamy, Ann and Nancy Robins, Bernard Miner, Chet, Let and Kahleen Schrader, Mary Ann and Garnet Kinney, Larry Denton, Harry and Gayle Knox, Duane, Mary, Jean, Barbara and Larry Westermelt, Michael Sullivan, Tony and Mary Jo Mastasa, Nancy Schutter. Other classmates over the years included Jim Wilcox, Jean and Joan Kinney, Dick Finley, Billy Pearsal, Lois Knox, Earl, Harold and Leroy Schutter, Beaulah, Patty and Dick Wert, Ron Benton, Ester Benton, and Neil and Sharon Butler.

Hillman School 1946 Class
Back Row: Frank Davis, Madeline Wert, Nancy Schutter, Mary Ellen Ellis, LeRoy Schutter, Tom Ellis, Jean Kinney, Bernard Miner, Mickey Denton, Mrs. Lenora Taft, Lois Knox, Joan Kinney, Barbara Nienhuis, Harold Schutter
Front Row: Beulah Wert, Chester Schrader, Lester Schrader, Larry Denton, Beverly Bellamy, Mary Anne Kinney, Dick Finley, Harry Knox, Dale Bellamy, Esther Benton, David Wert

Hillman School 1949 Class
Back Row: Mickey Denton, Jim Wilcox, David Wert, Bernard Miner, Barbara
Nienhuis, Esther Benton, Nancy Schutter, Mrs. Eloise Norquist
Middle Row: Beverly Bellamy, Chester Schrader, Lester Schrader, Harry Knox,
Larry Denton, Beulah Wert, Dale Bellamy
Front Row: Eugene Bellamy, Ronnie Bellamy, Garnet Kinney, Beulah Wert,
Gayle Knox, Michael Sullivan

Memories of Esther (Benton) Collard

Esther (Benton) Collard attended Hillman School from Kindergarten to eighth grade during the years 1941 to 1949. Esther is the daughter of Ronald and Esther Benton who lived on Cypress Avenue near the school. She remembers playing softball and red rover on the playground and the students performing the annual Christmas program. Her teachers were Miss Bryant, Nora Mast, Ms. Taft, and Mrs. Norquist. Some of the teachers boarded with the Benton family during the school year. During Esther's school years, the students used outhouses as there was no indoor plumbing. After her eighth grade graduation, Esther traveled by bus to attend high school. Other children who attended Hillman School during the 1940s included the names of Kinney, Knox, Ellis, Slott, Denton, Schrader, Schutter and Wert.

Hillman School 1950 Class
Back Row: Bernard Miner, Nancy Schutter, Duane Westervelt, Larry Denton,
*   Lester Schrader, Chester Schrader, Harry Knox, Mrs. Esther Benton*
Middle Row: Beverly Bellamy, Mary Anne Kinney, Mary Lou Westervelt, Nancy
*   Robbins, Ann Robbins, Joann Westervelt, Eugene Bellamy, Gayle Knox,*
*   Dale Bellamy*
Front Row: Beulah Wert, Garnet Kinney, Patty Wert, Ronnie Bellamy, Mary Jo
*   Nastasi, Kathleen Schrader, Barbara Westervelt, Larry Westervelt,*
*   Tony Nastasi, Michael Sullivan*

July 31, 1941 Newaygo Republican News Article

165 former pupils and teachers of Hillman School gathered Sunday at Baptist Lake for the first reunion of the group to meet every year after.

Officers elected were Franklin Denton, President and Raymond Shattuck, Secretary-Treasurer.

Seven former teachers were present including Neil Dunworth of Morley, Mable Kinney Myers and Blanche Seigel of Sand Lake, Erma Sage, Mary Crofoot Buitdendyker and Fanny O'Flynn Davidson, all of Grand Rapids, and Beatrice Bryant of Pierson. One of the oldest teachers who was unable to attend was Mrs. Kit Hillman of Grand Rapids.

Oldest pupils that were in attendance were Tom Kinney of Baptist Lake, Mrs. Ed Mathews of Rockford and William Shattuck of Ensley.

Hillman School 1951 Class
Standing: Mr. Ronald Benton, unknown, Eugene Bellamy, Beverly Bellamy,
*   Ann Robbins, Dale Bellamy, Bernard Miner, Mary Anne Kinney,*
*   Nancy Robbins.*
Sitting with instruments: Larry Denton, Lester Schrader, Harry Knox, Chester
*   Schrader, Duane Westevelt*
Other students: Garnet Kinney, Michael Sullivan, Kathleen Schrader, Mary Jo
*   Nastasi, Joann Westervelt, Barbara Westervelt, Tony Nastasi, unknown,*
*   Mary Lou Westervelt, Nancy Schutter, Larry Westervelt, Ron Bellamy*

Memories of Lorraine Slott Bull

My parents were John Ralph Slott and Alice Helen Gibson Slott and we lived at 7767 104th Street, Howard City. (However, during those years the address was simply RR #1, Howard City. It wasn't until later that house numbers were issued and the road was named.)

I attended Hillman School from Beginners (we never heard the word Kindergarten) until we moved to Muskegon when I was in 5th grade. (Dad had quit farming and got a job in a defense factory.)

I was allowed to start school when I was 4 years old. The reason for this was my older sister Evelyn did not want to go to school as there was a man teacher at Hillman at that time. Our neighbor boy, Frank Hillman, an 8th grader, would come each morning to walk to school with Evelyn. However, once they reached the point I the road where she could no longer peek over her shoulder and see our house, Evelyn would begin to cry, break away from Frank and run home. If only there hadn't been that man teacher, as Evelyn really did love school. In fact, her favorite pastime was rounding up our younger sister, brother and me and making us her pupils and spending endless hours "teaching" us.

On the other hand, man teacher or not, I was begging to attend school. Finally, the teacher consulted with my parents, and the following fall I was allowed to go. After that, Evelyn assumed the roll of big sister and hand in hand we walked the three-quarters of a mile to Hillman.

The year span I was at Hillman was from 1937 through the fall of 1941.

The school was named for Frank Hillman, the grandfather of our neighbor boy. Hillman School still stands.

My typical lunch consisted of sandwiches of homemade bread with homemade butter, homemade jam, jelly or meatloaf, also homemade cookies or a piece of homemade cake, plus, an apple, or occasionally, an orange. (We loved it when we had an orange as Alberta Brace, a big girl at school, always ate everyone's orange peelings!) I also carried a small bottle of vanilla milk. How well I remember that cute little bottle that the vanilla extract came in. It was a pretty shape and had a little ear. Mother would fill the bottle with milk and add some sugar and a dab of vanilla. I loved the smell and taste of vanilla and was always pestering Mother to add more to my lunch bottle. One day when Mother was working in the garden I was thirsty and coaxed Mother to make me some vanilla milk but she was too busy. Ah! I saw my opportunity! I'd make my own vanilla milk. And I did. With lots and lots of vanilla! Naturally, it was undrinkable. I learned my lesson—a little vanilla goes a long way!

One more thought about food. The first night we moved to Muskegon Mother knew she wouldn't have time to make bread so she stopped at Food City on Western Avenue in Muskegon and bought "store bread." We kids thought the "boughten" bread was simply wonderful! But it didn't take us long to get over that novelty, and we were thankful to have homemade bread again.

Here are some of the games I remember playing: Giant's Den, Stoop Tag, Mother May I?, Annie-i-over-the-woodshed, various ball games and Fox and Geese. In the winter we'd bring our sleds to school and slide down the hill across the road from school. In the springtime, Miss Bryant would take us on a long Nature Walk in the neighboring woods.

Sister Evelyn remembers one Easter when the shades in the school room were drawn and the 8th graders hid Easter baskets on the playground for the younger ones to find.

Without a doubt the most special program of the year was the annual Christmas program. Not only did all of us kids have pieces to learn, parts in the plays, Christmas songs, etc., but we made piles of red and green paper chains. The "big boys" on step ladders strung the chains between the hanging lights. (We did not have electricity in our home nor did most of the families in our school. However, the road going north from Ensley Center had electric poles and Hillman School was electrified. It had four large round fixtures hanging on long chains from the high ceiling.)

The Christmas program most clear in my mind is this one. Miss Bryant put a large, round washtub on chairs and Elinor Pratt, Ron Bentor and I sat in that tub. We chanted the poem "Rub-a-dub-dub three men in a tub, the butcher, the baker and the candlestick maker." There was more to the poem, but I can't remember the rest. I do remember the beautiful, green, satin dress I wore to that program. My little Swedish grandma, Emma Gibson, had been a tailoress in Sweden and she kept us supplied with pretty aprons and dresses. These were often made from clothing discarded by her two school teacher daughters. Sister Evelyn remembers that same program. She had a battered doll and recited the poem "Evangline has lost an eye, Marie had long an arm, (? can't remember next line). If we wore out like dollies do, how sad my mother'd be. She'd have to get another girl to take the place of me."

Whenever there was a "doings" at the schoolhouse, the building was packed! Before the age of TV, folks pretty much made their own entertainment and a program at the school was not to be missed. Everyone in the neighborhood attended whether or not they had children in school. We students were packed into the entryway and the cloak rooms as the parents and guests filled our seats and desks and lined the walls.

Miss Beatrice Bryant (later she married a Mr. Paulson) was my teacher through the 4th grade. She was a wonderful teacher and we loved her very much. Miss Nora Mast, an old lady, was my teacher for a couple of months that fall I was in 5th grade. Miss Mast had come out of retirement as it was War time and many of the men teachers had been drafted.

Miss Race was our music teacher. I don't remember how often she came nor on what day of the week. I do remember she was very thin and that she got into trouble. Apparently she was against the War effort and, as a result, she taught us kids to sing "I don't want to march in the infantry, ride in the cavalry, shoot the artillery. I don't want to fly over Germany. I want to be friendly."

I remember going to "Field Day" at the town of Sand Lake. We walked down Main Street and the various merchants gave us little trinkets and/or candy treats. My Uncle Clayton Simpson was part owner of the local hardware store "Sinclair and Simpson" and Oh, My! Was I ever proud when Uncle greeted us kids and then paid special attention to me. After our little one-room school the "big" Sand Lake school building really impressed us kids. We were fascinated with the gigantic fire escape that was on one side of the building. It was a huge, round, pipe-like-thing that extended from the 3rd story down to the ground. Miss Bryant and we kids rode to the Sand Lake doings in Mr. Rynard's open cattle truck. (Evelyn can't remember this, but I don't think I dreamed it!)

Hillman School had two outhouses—boys and girls. We raised two fingers when we wanted permission to go to the toilet. (One raised finger was to speak to another pupil, and our raised hand meant we needed the teacher's attention.) Here is an outhouse memory. One of the naughty boys dug a trench behind the girls' outhouse and crawled into it. Then he bragged on the playground how he could look up and see our bare bottoms hanging in the hole. Once his antics reached Miss Bryant's ears, she soon put a stop to it!

The following memory happened when Miss Bryant lost her key to the schoolhouse. It was the only key to the building. For several days all of us children and our teacher had to crawl through a window to get in and out of the building. We had to climb on a chair to reach the window. The boys thought it was great fun, but we girls were embarrassed. All girls wore dresses in those days—no slacks or jeans—and we had a hard time keeping our dresses and underskirts under control as we climbed over the windowsill. What a terrible thing if some boy were to see our underpants!

For a while there was some sort of hot lunch program at Hillman School. I'm thinking this may have begun when I was in 4th grade. I do remember Rose Peterson coming to our school occasionally and making soup. It didn't go over too great with me perhaps that's why I don't remember much about it. It wasn't that the soup wasn't good or that I was a fussy eater but, rather, that I was spoiled by my mom's super good cooking. Also, on some days the school mothers brought in food.

World War II became a very real and scary thing for the Hillman School kids when one day at recess time a mother came driving up to the schoolhouse. There were a couple little ones in the car with her and the mother and the children were all crying. She had just been notified that her soldier boy son had been killed in the War. The mother had come to take her school-age children home. It was a sad and solemn day for all of us. (The name of this family slips my mind right now.)

This is Lorraine Slott Bull's all-time favorite Valentine which was given to by her teacher Miss Bryant

Valentine from Miss Bryant to Lorraine Slott

Some favorite Valentines received by Lorraine Slott Bull from her classmates

From Charles Brace

From Wava Denton

From Leon Shattuck
The valentine came with a
sucker attached to it.

From Gerald Knox

From Leon Shattuck

Hillman School Students
Front row (left to right): Shirley Wood, Mary Ellen Ellis, Lorraine Slott, Elinor Pratt,
Lois Knox
Back row: Carl? Brace, Ron Benton, Wava Denton, Evelyn Slott, Bob Ellis (peeking
over his shoulder), George Pratt, Patsy Brace.

Hillman School
Students
Front row (left to
right): Esther Ben-
ton, Joan and Jean
Kinney, Mary Ellen
Ellis, unknown
Back row: Un-
known, Ron Ben-
ton, Lois Knox,
Elinor Pratt, Shirley
Wood

Hillman School Students
(Lorraine Slott Bull's favorite school picture)
Front row (left to right): Carl Brace, Ron Benton, Mary Ellen Ellis, George Pratt,
Charles Brace, Wava Denton, Patsy Brace, Lorraine Slott, Elinor Pratt,
Ruthann Brace, Lois Knox (center front)
Back row: Bob Ellis, Barbara Brace, Carmen Grove Bennett, Alberta Brace,
Evelyn Slott, Gerald Knox, Miss Bryant

Hillman School
Students
Front row (left to
right): Elinor Pratt,
Lorraine Slott, Ron
Benton, unknown,
unknown (note bare
feet), Shirley Wood,
Wava Denton, Gerald
Knox
Center row: George
Pratt, unknown, Ev-
elyn Slott, Bob Ellis
Back row: Carmen

Grove Bennett, unknown, unknown, unknown, Barbara Denton, unknown, Miss
Bryant

Hillman School Students
Front row (left to right): Lorraine Slott, Gerlad Knox, Wava Denton, unknown,
*   Shirley Wood*
Center row: Carl Lapree, Evelyn Slott, unknown, unknown, unknown, George Pratt
Back row: Miss Bryant, unknown, unknown, Barbara Denton, unknown, unknown

Hillman School students
Frank Hillman on the left

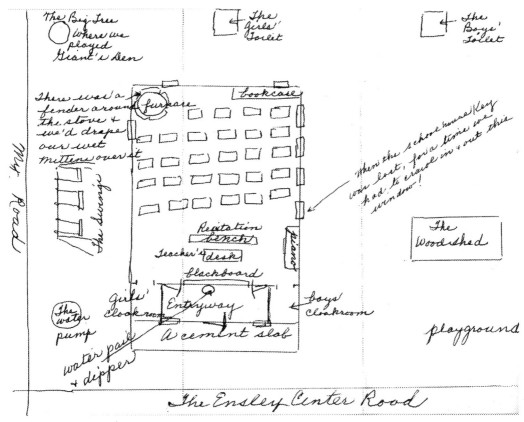

The Big Tree Where we played Giant's Den

The Girls' Toilet

The Boys' Toilet

There was a fender around the stove & we'd drape our wet mittens over it

furnace

bookcase

When the schoolhouse Key was lost, for a time we had to crawl in & out this window!

The Wood shed

Mur. Road

the divange

Recitation bench

Teacher's desk

Blackboard

piano

The water pump

Girls' cloakroom

Entryway

boys cloakroom

playground

water pail + dipper

A cement slab

The Ensley Center Road

Layout of Hillman School drawn by Lorraine Slott Bull

Hillman School student working at her desk next to the battered old furnace that kept the students warm and dried their mittens.

"The Ball Game"
**Hillman School students playing ball on the playground. Note in the background the
woodshed (left) where the students played "Annie-i-over" and the boys toilet.**

**This is a photo copy of a large oil painting Lorraine Slott Bull made of Hillman
School. The painting is titled "The Night of the Christmas Program."**

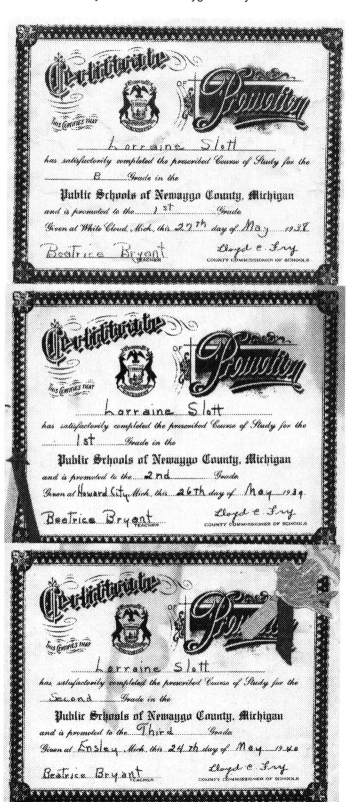

Lorraine Slott's Certificate of Promation from Beginners through 2nd Grade

Newaygo County Public Schools

Teacher's Report to Parent

Pupil _Lorraine Slott_

School _Hillman_   Grade _1_

Dist. _2_   Twp. _Ensley_

For School Year Ending _____ 193_9_

Miss Bryant
Teacher

Lloyd C. Fry
County Commissioner of Schools

Method of Grading
- A—Excellent
- B—Very Good
- C—Good
- D—Fair
- E—Failure
- I—Incomplete

STUDIES	1	2	3	Av	4	5	6	Av
Arithmetic	B	B	C-	B	B-	B		
Arts	A	A	A	A	A	A		
English								
History								
Health								
Penmanship	C	B	A	B	B	B		
Reading	B	B	C-	B	B	B		
Spelling	B	B	C	B	B	B		
Geography								
Science								
Civil Gov't								
Music			C					

TRAITS OF PUPIL

Attitude Toward School Work	1	2	3	4	5	6
Intensive Worker						
Wastes Time						
Depends on Others						
Self-reliant						
Persistent						
Shows Improvement						
Very Commendable					✓	

TRAITS OF PUPIL
Recitations

Attitude Toward School Work	1	2	3	4	5	6
Well Prepared						
Effort Good						
Responsive						
Inattentive				✓	✓	
Attentive						
Promotion in Danger						
Capable of Doing Better						
Work of Grade Difficult						
Shows Improvement						
Satisfactory					✓	
Exceptionally Good						

Conduct

	1	2	3	4	5	6
Courteous						
Mischievous						
Cooperates with Teacher						
Shows Improvement						
Satisfactory					✓	
Very Good						

Attendance

	1	2	3	4	5	6
Half Days Present			87	46	96	
Half Days Absent			12	14	14	
Times Tardy			1	3		

Lorraine Slott's Report Card from 1939

Hillman School Students 1926
1st row: Raymond Tawney, Raymond Boyd, Edan Pratt, Gordon Bohn
2nd row: Bernie Olsen, Colon Pratt, Naomi Waller, John Boyd, Thelma Tawney, teacher
*   Clare Dunworth*
3rd row: Ruth Tawney Maurer, Mary Tawney, Dorothy Schuede, Allen Bellamy,
*   Lawrence Weller*
4th row: Eleanor Bohn, Chester Lockard, Oliver Bellamy, Forrest Bohn, Robert Tawney

Hillman School
Students circa 1925
1st row: C.L.
Goodwell, Allen Bel-
lamy, Casey Jones
(Don), Alfred Colin
Pratt
*   2nd row: Gor-*
don Bohn, Ella
Goodwell, Doris
Hillman, Mary
Tawney, Norma
Hillman, Thelma
Tawney, Doris
Waller, ? Goodwell.
3rd row: Laurence Waller, Robert Tawney, Forrest Bohn, Darrel Staley, Nelda Butler,
Dorothy Schrader, Naomi Waller. Teacher: Neil Dunworth

Hillman School Students 1889-1890
Minnie Washer Meyers is in first from the right in front. Her sister Libby is behind her, third from the right.
John Welch, showing off his new boots, is in the front row, fourth from the left.
Willie Welch is in the front row, seventh from the left.
Last names of other students who attended Hillman School include: Brooks, Van Liew, Matthews, Hillman, Lieujen, Kelly, Schrader, Terwilliger, and Bellamy.

October 8, 1903 – Newaygo Republican
Hillman School, #2 Ensley reports: Pupils not absent during the month ending Oct. 2 - Rosie, Olive and Fanny Flynn, Allie and Eugene Hillman, Mabel and Veronica Kinney, Lyle Randall. Sadie Kinney, Teacher.

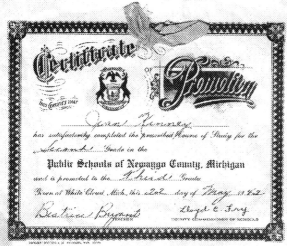

Jean Kinney's Certificates of Class Promotion Jean's sister Joan contributed several of the class and reunion photos for Hillman School.

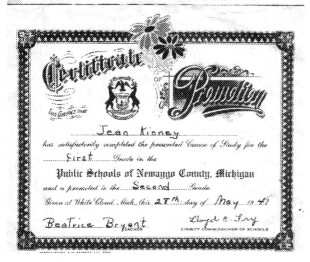

Teacher Alice Swanson
1953

Teacher Joy Brisbin
1953

Teachers Eloise Norquist & Beatrice Bryant Paulsen
at the 2000 Hillman School Reunion

Burnice L. Pickerd's 8th grade diploma 1936

1954 Hillman School Reunion at Kinney's Grove, Baptist Lake
Back Row: Lee Denton, Ira Perry, John Shattuck, Ed Kelley, Raymond Shattuck,
Bill Goerner, Oliver Bellamy, Eugene Hillman, Tom Kinney, Don Kinney,
Frank Terwilliger, John Welch, John Loftus, Edmund Schrader, George
Welch, Neil Dunworth, Leonard Tawney, Ed Siegel
Middle Row: Leona Denton, Bernice Knop, Veronica Perry, Marie Shattuck, Ellen
Welch, Frances Davison, Carrie Dunworth, Mabel Tift, Joan Kinney,
Evelyn Slott, Joan Slott, Mary Anne Kinney, Clayton Brown, David Ellis
Front Row: Roma Welch, Helen Goerner, Maxine Donaldson, Florence Jones,
Betty Shattuck, Leona Bellamy, Fern Kinney, Vera Knox, Olive Loftus,
Mamie Kelley, Ella Ellis, Alice Slott, Elma Hillma, Garnet Kinney,
Donna Kinney, Blanche Siegel

1993 Hillman School Reunion at Ensley Grange Hall
Back Row: Dale Bellamy, Melvin Bellamy, Carol Jean Bellamy, Beulah Wert, Esther Benton, Mary Anne Kinney, Garnet Kinney, Daryl Brace, Jim Schutter, David Wert
Middle Row:

Joan Slott, Beverly Bellamy, Shirley Wood, Edith Schutter, Lorraine   Slott, Eleanor Pratt, Edna Pratt, Mary Ellen Ellis
Front Row: Jean Kinney, Joan Kinney, Evelyn Slott, Mrs. Eloise Norquist, Mr. Ronald Benton, Miss Beatrice Bryant, Bob Ellis, Leon Shattuck, Colin Pratt

2000 Hillman School Reunion at Ensley Grange Hall
Back Row: Leon Shattuck, Colin Pratt, Edith Schutter, George Pratt, Eddie Pratt, Milford Pratt, Ron Benton, Leroy Schuter
Middle Row: Loraine Slott, Garnet Kinney, Mary Ellen Ellis, Patty Wert, Darlene Wert, David

Wert, Forest Bohn, Cindy Bohn
Front Row: Evelyn Slott, Joan Kinney, Mary Anne Kinney, Miss Beatrice Bryant, Jean Kinney, Mrs. Eloise Norquist, Elinor Pratt, Leon Pratt

Kinney School

Kinney School
School District No. 7

Kinney School, named after the Kinney family, was located in Section 11 at the corner of 112th Street and Beech.

John and Mary (McCue) Kinney and family came to Ensley Township in 1856. Their children were Thomas, James, Maria, John Jr., Pat, Kathryn, and Michael. Several of the Kinney descendants were teachers and taught in Newaygo County schools. Each of the nine schools in Ensley Township had at least one Kinney descendant as a teacher and between 1885 and 1920 there was a Kinney descendant teaching in at least one Ensley Township school.

Kinney descendants that were teachers included Mabel Kinney, Veronica Kinney, Mary Kinney, Ellen Kinney, Theresa Kinney, Dora Kinney, Rose Kinney, Nora Kinney, Arthur Kinney, Sadie Kinney, Kathryn Kinney, Elizabeth Kinney, Francis Kinney, Florence Kinney, Minnie Kinney, Blanche Welch, and Mariel (Welch) Siegel.

The school closed in the 1930s or 1940's.

Teachers: Kathryn Kinney – circa 1906 (was paid $256 for the year), Donna Harden (1913), Gladys Douglas (1917), Murriel Tiffany (1919), Earl Gallister (1926-27)

1917 graduates: Clayton Simpson, Lucy Patin
1919 graduates: Alfred Hackbardt and Walter Hackbardt

Kinney School as it looked a few years after it had closed.

*Kinney School
1913 Class*

*Front row:
Edith John-
son, Hildred
Schmidt, Orpha
Cain, Harold
Hills, Leonard
Newland, Walter
Hackbardt, Alfred
Hackbardt, John
Johnson, William
Johnson*

    *2nd row: Freda
Newberg, Iva Hills, Esther Schmidt, Hazel Hackbardt, Bertha Bradley, Lyle Holmes,
Sam Newberg, Uleric Newland*
    *3rd row: Dan Schmidt, Florence Cain, Nelie Hills, Albert Newland, Albert Johan-
son, Lena Saiter, Teacher Donna Harden, Frank Schmidt, Earl Bradley, Frank Cain*

*Kinney School
1926-27 Class*

*Front row:
Winona Holmes,
Donna Miles,
Irene Meginley,
Jack? Weaver,
Glen Meginley,
Donna Megin-
ley, Junior Zenk
    2nd row:
Herbert John-
son, George
Norwood, Edna
Newland, Grace
Miles, Ernest*

Johnson, Harold Newland, Willie Griffes, Margarite Griffes
    *3rd row: Iva Griffes, Hazel Johnson, Sarah Norwood, Teacher Earl Gallister, Leo
Griffes, Charles Johnson*

Pangborn School
School District No. 4 (aka 8)

Pangborn school was also known as the East School because it was on the east side of the township. The school was located in Section 34 at the corner of 136th Street and Cypress.

The school was named after the Pangborn family who moved to the area in the 1850's. Pangborn Corners was located on the border for Newaygo and Montcalm counties and Elisha Pangborn built a store there in the 1860's. Elisha was elected sheriff of Newaygo County in 1879 and his son, B.W. Pangborn ran the store while he was in office.

Teachers: Sadie Kinney (circa 1900), Harry Spooner (circa 1906), Mr. Branyon (1917), Jennie Fidler (1919), Mr. Mellon (1959), Bertha Hayward (1962-63)

Pangborn School

Pangborn School Class April 1891
Front row: Lizzie Fisk, Fred Udell, Anna Yost, Ella Heath, Lula Carroll, Mary Yost,
    Darwin Gilbert, Glenn Willis, Fred Siegel, Frank Siegel, Elmer Harvey,
    Johnny Thorn, ? Brown, Theodore Reuben Brownyard, Ralph Carroll,
    Herbert Maynard and Frank Hart.
2nd row: Janie Thorn, Rubie Brown, Gertie Maynard, Mable Hart, Allie McQueen,
    Alice Willis Sadie Cook.
Back row: Rettie Lord, Nora Hart, Nettie Cook, Lura Salsgiver, Alta Randall,
    Alta Wheeler, Mamie Siegle, teacher Florence Fisk.

Pangborn School Class 1940

Spring Valley School was remodeled into a home as you can
see by this photo taken in the 1980's.

Spring Valley School
School District No. 4

Spring Valley School was named after the spring of water that it was near. It was located in Section 20 on 120th Street just east of Locust.

Closed in 1941 due to decrease in number of students and the few students were sent to Ensley Center School. The school reopened in 1946 when student population increased.

In 1900 the average number of students enrolled at Spring Valley School was 28.

Teachers: A.R. Alger (1900), LeRoy Cochrane (1901), Flossie Bigelow (1919), Dora Brydges (1938), Nora Jean (1959), Marlene Ann Miller (1961-62)

1919 graduates: Rachel Norquist, Hazel Nelson and Mabel Gibson

*Spring Valley
School Class
Circa 1925*

*Front row:
Richard Sim-
mons, Willis
Simmons, Sam
Butler, John
Nelson, Cecil
Bergman
2nd row:
Marion Crispin,
Myrtle Crispin,
Mildred Schu-
maker, Nellie
Butler
3rd row:
Irving Schumaker, Ivan Gibson, Teacher Rachel Norquist, Fannie Bergman, Hazel
Crispin*

*Spring Valley School Class 1934
Teacher - Eloise Carlson
Front row: Harry Nelson, Colleen Crispin, John Johnson, Florene Butler,
Betty Johnson, Eloise Crispin
Back row: Roger Butler, Gerald Nagelhout, Olive Jones, Carl Nelson, Martin
Johnson, Marian Crispin, Kathryn Johnson, Lela Marvin, Evelyn Shears*

Everett Township

Everett Township was one of the earliest townships established in Newaygo County. It was created in 1856 by splitting Big Prairie Township in two. At that time it encompassed an area six miles across and twenty-four miles long. The township changed shape many times before it became the size that it is known today. It is designated as Township 13 North, Range 12 West.

In 1880 the township had five whole school districts and one fractional district with about 163 students attending school. Six of the school houses were frame built and one was a log building. There were eight teachers (one male and seven female).

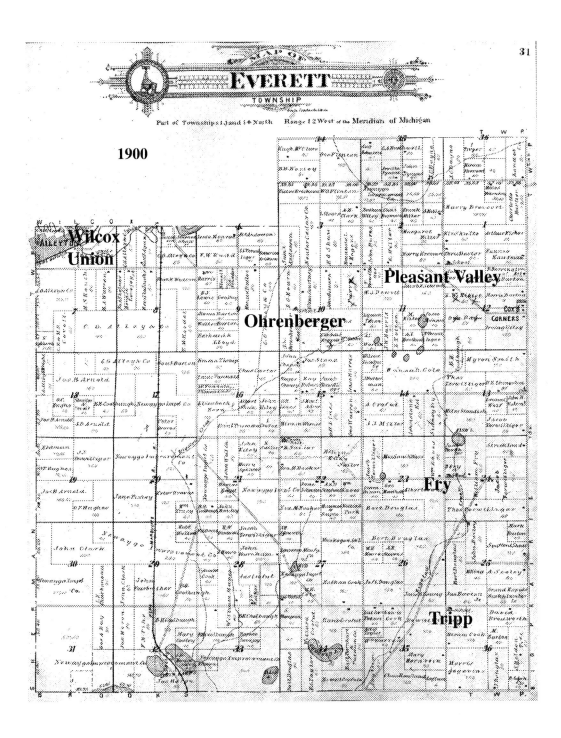

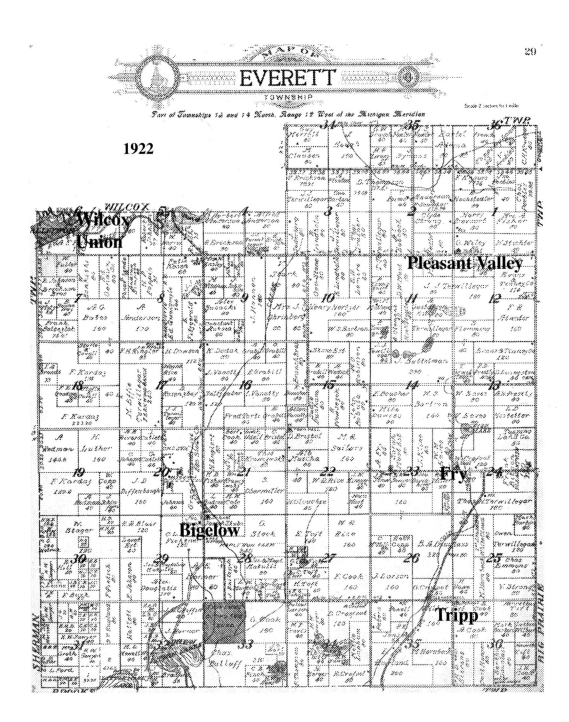

1922

Bigelow School
School District #2

Bigelow School was located in Section 28 and was named for Bigelow Creek which flowed behind the school. The school consolidated with White Cloud Public Schools in the fall of 1959.

June 13, 1895 - Newaygo Republican

School District 2, Everett Township, report for term ending June 6. 14 pupils enrolled. Pupils not absent: Hilda Riley, Minnie Riley, Otis Boyd, Mabel Boyd, Pearl Riley, Dora Riley. Emma Thompson, Teacher.

Bigelow School was sold to Henry and Flo Ballast in the early 1980's and they remodelled it into a home.

Memories of Earl Page

Earl Page, son of John and Florence Page, who lived on 24th Street in Everett Township. Earl attended Bigelow Creek School in the late 1930's and remembers walking the one and one half miles to school in any and all kinds of weather. There was no such thing as a snow day.

The neighbor children, which included the Davis, Craigmyle and Page families, would all walk together. Ethel Stock was the only teacher he had until he transferred to the White Cloud School in 1942. Ethel Stock lived on Walnut Ave. about a half mile from the school.

There was a total of 22 to 25 students each year covering grades Kindergarten to eighth grade. Each morning started with saying the Pledge of Allegiance, a silent prayer, and a verse from the Bible. The regular subjects usually started with reading first with math, language arts and social studies in the afternoon. The kids always looked forward to the Christmas programs, especially when they were let out of school to practice their plays.

After attending Bigelow School, Earl went to the White Cloud school in 1942 and graduated at age 17. He worked at Briggs Lumber Company to earn the money to attend the County Normal School. The County Normal School was a college for those who wanted to be certified as teachers.

Earl began his teaching career in 1956, first teaching at Wayland before coming back to Newaygo County and teaching at several schools including Donahue, Brookside, Bitely, Roottown, and Oak Grove Schools. His remembers that it was stipulated in his contract that he would have a silent prayer and say one Bible verse at the beginning of each school day.

During the colder months, Earl would begin each day by stoking the coal furnace in the morning and would always bank it up before leaving. It was much easier after an oil furnace was installed and the heat could be maintained by a thermostat. The oil furnace and controlled heat also meant that bathrooms could be installed inside the school house instead of having to use outhouses outside. The school was the center of the community's activities. Several gatherings were held throughout the year when all the families would come together to enjoy good food and socialize. The biggest event of the year was always at Christmas time. The kids all brought their own lunches to school and every Friday was trade-off day where they would exchange food items with other kids. When the weather got warmer, all the children who had reached their goals for the week would be allowed to play softball. They would often play against other schools in the area. Earl also remembered one winter blizzard when a tractor and wagon was used to get the kids home from school.

Memories of Truax family

In 1950 Robert and Betty Truax built a house at Rt. #1 Box 40, White Cloud. They moved in with their five children, David, Florence, Ann, James, William and Kathaleen. Dave, Ann and Jim went to Bigelow Creek School that year. Bill and Kathy were too young. Patricia was born the following year. When old enough, Bill, Kathy and Pat also attended school there.

Mrs. Tanis and Mrs. Lila Alger are the teachers that we remember.

The three oldest children graduated 6th grade and then went into White Cloud to the old high school. Each graduating class was sent on a special trip. Dave was privileged to go to the Mackinaw Bridge. Ann and Jim went to Kellogg factory and an arboretum in Battle Creek. The last three of us, Bill, Kathy and Pat, didn't get to graduate from there. At the end of the 1959 school year, they consolidated our school and sent us to White Cloud Public Schools. Kathy and Bill had finished 3rd grade. I [Pat] had finished 2nd grade. Entering a school that big was the most terrifying thing we had ever been forced to do.

Betty, my mother, and Ramona, my grandmother, used to prepare the lunch meal in the school basement. I [Pat] remember being too young to attend school, but still going there with my grandmother. We rode with the milkman on rainy days. We walked on the pleasant days. The school was a half mile from our home. I was allowed to play in the sandbox in the coat room. I also sat at a table in the basement watching her prepare the meal. I was allowed to sit in back of the classroom if I was quiet. This was my favorite choice. This was all before I was old enough to attend school.

After one summer vacation, we arrived to find that bees had taken up residence under the eave at the front door. It was a very large nest. We all had to enter from the rear of the school until it could be removed. The big boys were caught throwing things at the nest.

The Bigelow Creek ran right behind the school. It was quite a drop to reach it. In the winter, the students, mostly boys, would slide down the hill on shovels. More than one ended their ride in the creek. Usually it was frozen over.

Bigelow Creek School building is still standing tall. It is now a private residence.

Other family names we remember from our one-room school house: Ringler, Borkowski, Nowak, Goodson, Davis, Dutcher, McCumber, Schafer.

Memories of Phyllis (Davis) Green

Phyllis, daughter of Chauncey and Virginia Davis, lived along M-37 and attended Bigelow Creek School from Kindergarten through the 6th grade (1943-1950). Her early lunches consisted of a sandwich, cookies, and milk. Later, her mother came and cooked hot meals at the school. Recess games included King of the Mountain, Red Rover, Got to the corner & pass, baseball, and Simon Sez. The children used outhouses for restrooms.

"I loved going to school at Bigelow Creek. When it was time for me to go to 'town school,' I really did not want to go. We walked to and from school every day unless it was rainy or snowing too hard, then Grandpa took us.

"I think my fondest memory of a special event at our country school was Christmas. We students worked for days stringing popcorn with a needle and thread. We would cut colored strips of paper in 5" to 6" strips, about 1" wide. These were all colors: blue, yellow, green, white, pink, and sometimes, red and blue if our teacher could get these colors. Afternoons were spent gluing the strips in circles, connecting them together to form a chain. This tree was decorated with all homemade ornaments. One year Teacher brought small candle holders and we had a tree lighted with real candles.

"For weeks we would practice our parts for the Christmas play, and all the songs we would be singing. Finally, the big night was here! Everyone had a part in the play, so everyone's family came. I especially remember my Father...he was a great singer, and he sang every song at those Christmas programs.

"If we had to go to the outhouse, I can still remember how beautiful our school looked

Members of the Davis family

The windows all lit with the lights from the tree, the decorations we had put in the windows, and the folks inside singing Christmas carols.

"Oh, to be able to go back to the 'good old days' so our children would be able to see how we celebrated Christmas."

Her teachers were Ethel Stock, Nettie Mast and Alice Swanson. Her classmates were Ruth, Ila, Phyllis, Darrel, August and Nancy Davis; Peter, Eloise, Larry and Marvel Davis; Dick, Bud, Wayne, Chuck, Jim and Butch Flinton; Irene, Virginia, Fred, Bernice, Doris, Carol Wally, Peggy and Matt Borkowski; Frances and Sharon Nowak; Margaret, June and Donald Dutcher; Norman and Willis Clary; Alberta, Andrew and Reuben Jackson; Bill, Pat, Joe and Ben Aishe; Thelma Swoveland; Wesley Raines; Bonnie, David, Lloyd and Keith Wismar; David, Kathy, Anna, James and Bill Truax.

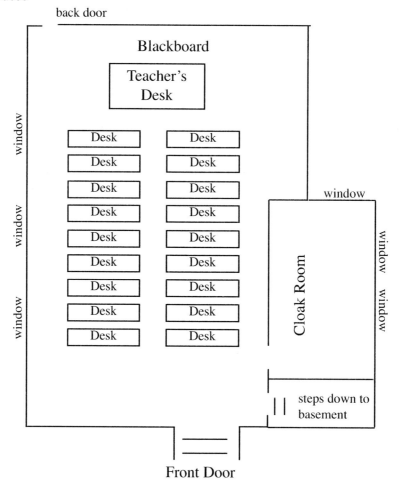

Layout of Bigelow Creek Schoolhouse
remembered by Phyllis (Davis) Green

Fry School

Fry School
School District #1

This school was originally known as the Slade School in its first location, south of Bitson's Corners on Pine Street. It was not uncommon for a one-room schoolhouse to be moved from one location to another, and the Slade School was no exception. William and Philandia Fry donated land on the corner of Oak and 28th Street, and so the former Slade School became the Fry School sometime in the 1880's when it was moved to its new home.

In May of 1959, Fry School consolidated into the White Cloud Public Schools, and the students of Fry School were bussed to White Cloud, along with their current teacher, Howard Douglas.

The Fry School building reverted to private ownership (date unknown), when Jerry and Helen Teegardin purchased the former school building and renamed it Fry Chapel. They held Sunday school classes there for many years, and the building still stands proudly today.

More facts about Fry School:

• At least six students were required to be in attendance in order for the school to open.

• School fund-raising--you think it was invented in the 21st century? Think again. Violet Babula remembered her 6th grade class sold Jello to raise money for a crank-type record player!

• Daily routines varied from grade to grade, but would have been similar to school today (on a basic level). The younger grades learned their letters or the alphabet (the Palmer writing method was commonly used). Some time during the day, the teacher would read a story aloud. The older or "bigger" boys had the daily chore of keeping the woodbox filled and ashes dumped outside. (Incidentally, "naughty" or bad boys were not invented with our generation. They plagued teachers even back then.)

Lunches consisted of whatever the students' family had on hand for them to bring, such as sandwiches (made with homemade bread). Filling for the sandwich was optional, such as peanut butter, mustard, bacon grease, or some type of meat. There were always apples, homemade soup (which could be warmed up on the woodstove), and occasionally, cookies.

Games at recess ran the gamut from soccer, softball, hide and seek, kick the can, tag, sledding, sheep my pen, gray wooly, and zippy.

Students back then did not get to go back to bed when there was a blizzard. You either made it or you didn't, but a "snow day" was never called. At Christmas time, there was usually a Christmas program or play along with recitations of certain "pieces" or poems that the children learned.

At the end of the year, there were exams and State mandated tests that students, hopefully, would pass to move on the next grade level. There was a special party on the last day of school.

Fry School Students
Front row: Unknown, Everett D.
2nd row: Louise Turner, Feral(sp?), Gladys
3rd row: Lloyd, Dan C., Eunice Myers, Gladys D.
Back row: Adrian S., Orson P., C. Fry, Cyril Waters, Ellsworth W.

Fry School Students Circa 1901
Teacher - Tom Nelson
Front row: Erwin Clemens, Elsie Mast, Alma Fry, Clara Terwillegar, Ruth
*   Terwillegar, John Henry Yoder, Ford Fry, Lyle Slade, Nathan Sailors*
Center row: Walter Eaves, Lilly Buttleman, Pearl Crofoot (above Lilly), Ila Warren,
*   Laura Sailors (dark dress), Harry VanGilder (card in cap), Alice Buttleman*
*   (behind Harry), Owen Terwillegar, Harry Fry, Fred Rowland (big boy*
*   without a cap), Ward Fry*
Back row: Clifton Meek, Charles Fry, Nancy Mast, Minnie Buttleman, Edith
*   Meek (behind card), Rose Mast, Clara Sailors, Jessie Sailors, Howard Slade,*
*   Morton Meek*

Fry School Teachers: Ruth Forwood-Maile, Howard Douglas, Neal Bowers (boarded with the Willard Crofoot family), Hazel Allers, Mary Waters, Greeta Timmer, Julia
Timmer, Tom Nelson (teaching contract for Sept. 2, 1901 to Jan. 30, 1902 for $25 per
month in Everett Twp. - He continued to teach in Newaygo County schools until 1914.)

Many of the teachers boarded with a local family, as they did not live in the area.

Memories of Raymond Boucher:

Felix and Lucille Boucher, Raymond's parents, lived on S. Poplar Avenue. Raymond attended Fry School from Kindergarten through the 8th grade (1938-1947). Sandwiches and cookies were a typical lunch and recess games were softball, hide and seek, sheep my pen and soccer. He walked two miles to school each day no matter what the weather as there were no snow days. His teacher was Howard Douglas and his classmates were Jack, Earl, and Francis Buttleman, Wayne Crofoot, Joe, Dorothy, and Jack McDonald, Dick, Bill and Jodi Matthews, LaVone Sailors, Raymond and Bernard Wawsczyk, Chris Aiseh, Mylas (Mike) Rudolph, Daisy Moore, Francis Trainer, Ruby Wolever (Bidelman), and the Morton family.

1942 Fry School students with teacher Howard Douglas

Memories of Raymond Wawsczyk:

Raymond lived on E. 20th Street with his parents, Roman and Agata Wawsczyk. He attended Fry School from 1941 to 1948 (Kindergarten through 6th grade). His lunches consisted of sandwiches (bacon grease) and apples when they were available. Games played were soccer, softball, zippy, gray wooly, kick the can, and hide and seek. The Christmas program was remembered for the recitation parts. The school had indoor plumbing and it had a large woodstove in the corner which heated the school. Howard Douglas was his only teacher. His classmates included Ruby (Bidelman) Wolever, Bernard Wawsczyk, Raymond Boucher, Shirley (Boucher) DeVries, Ruth (Gerencer) Troyanowski, Jeanette (Bitson) Harper, and many others who are now deceased.

Fry School Students Circa 1930
Front row: Neva Crofoot, Fern Crofoot, Mary Doring, Ina Evens, Jessie Bitson,
*   Germaine Boucher, Goldie Nelson, Anna Hoover*
Middle row: Noel Nelson, Lloyd Robinson, Felix Boucher, Joe Nelson, Tim Nelson,
*   Bill Koffman, Fred Bitson*
Back row: Velma Nelson, Jess Buttleman, Grace Bitson, Arthur Bitson, Bertha
*   Boucher, Dale Robinson (Arthur and Max Crofoot missing)*

Just the boys in the circa 1930 Fry School class
Felix Boucher is the 4th from the left in the white shirt.

1946 Fry School students with teacher Howard Douglas

Fry School students the Fall of 1946 with Teacher Howard Douglas

A photo of the Fry School in the 1980's.

Memories of Kenneth Roy Craigmyle:

Kenneth, son of Florence and Grover Craigmyle, lived along M-37 when he attended Fry School from 1950 to 1952 (4th through 6th grade). "I only attended for three years. As a kid I didn't pay a lot of attention." His lunches consisted of sandwiches of homemade bread, peanut butter and mustard. He remembered playing hide and seek, tag, ante-i-over, sheep my pen and sledding in winter. Memorable events were the Christmas program and the party on the last day of school. His teacher was Howard Douglas and his classmates were John Gerencer, Carol Gerencer, Wilma Boucher, Jenny Harper, Dick Wert, Tom Wert, Archie Wert, Verna Mead, Marion Price, Jody Matthews, Clifford Monroe, Ray Wawsczyk, Gloria Roeig (sp?), and Robin Price.

Fry School Teacher Howard Douglas

Howard Douglas taught school for 45 years teaching at Woodland Park, Forwood, Fry, and ending his career at White Cloud Elementary School. He was very active and well liked in his community. He joined the township fire department in 1973, serving as secretary-treasurer when he was no longer able to fight fires. He was the sexton of the Big Prairie-Everett Cemetery for many years as well. He and is wife Jessie were married for more than 56 years.

Memories of Violet Babula (1995)

Violet was born in East Chicago, Indiana and moved with her family to Everett Township in 1921. She started the 1st grade in 1925 at Fry School which was about a mile and half walk from her home. Her first grade teacher was Ruth Forwood Maile whom she remembered fondly. There were approximately six to eight students that year. Mrs. Maile would usually read a story every day and Violet liked it when she was the only one in her class due to the absence of Mamie Prestly and Robert Sutherland. On those days, Mrs. Maile would assign the older students their work for the day and then she would take Violet in her lap and read her a story.

When the weather was bad, Violet and Robert Sutherland would go home when the mail man, Ray Grabill, came around in his "cutter." He would share his bear blanket with the kids and usually produced a cookie for a treat.

Howard Douglas was Violet's 2nd grade teacher. Violet seemed to remember that there were a few more students that year. In particular, a family moved in near by that had a son named Paul who would give Violet and Mamie a "bad time." At Christmas that year, Mr. Douglas gave her a cup and saucer which she kept as a cherished memento.

Her 3rd grade teacher was Neal Bowers, who boarded with the Crofoot family. Every Friday afternoon, Mrs. Crofoot would come to the school and play the organ and the kids would sing songs and hymns.

Just before the end of the school year in 1928, Mamie Prestly came down with diptheria and the family was in quarantine. The school picnic was late that year and was held in Shaw Park in Newaygo.

Violet's teacher from 1928 to 1930 was Hazel Allers. Around that time, the three Websters, Alfred, Clifton and Esther, transferred to Fry School from Forwood School because they were the only students left in that school and six students were required before a school would open. Violet remembered that the "big boys" were a real trial for the teacher at times.

Mary Waters of Fremont was Violet's 6th grade teacher. That year, new families moved into the area to live and work in the woods. The student count that year was as high as 21. Over Christmas vacation, Miss Waters married Lacy Pennington. She boarded with the Crofoots during the week and her husband would pick her up on Fridays to go home for the weekend.

Violet's 7th grade teacher was Greeta Timmer of Fremont, who had just completed County Normal. Julia Timmer was the teacher the next year. The girls always admired the pretty dresses she wore. Violet couldn't remember a teacher ever being absent due to illness, but did remember that one day when Howard Douglas' brother Sidney was home from college, Howard took a day off and Sidney took a nap on the recitation bench and the students had a long recess that day.

Ohrenberger School
School District #5

The only information known about Ohrenberger School is that it was located in Section 10 of Everett Township and it was open in 1907. The school was closed before 1922.

Bertha Stone certificate admitting her to the 8th grade
in June 1909 at School District No. 5

Pleasant Valley School

Pleasant Valley School
School District #7

Pleasant Valley School was located in Section 1 on the northeast corner of 8th Street and Oak. In 1884 is was listed as School District #4.

Teachers: Eva Sackett (1884), Mrs. Waterman, Mrs. Graham

Students: Thomas Vickers, Conrad and Paul Thumser, Daniel, Norman and Martin Thompson

Memories of Lawrence Waybill

Lawrence Waybill lived on 8th Street and was the son of Viola Waybill. He attended Pleasant Valley School from Kindergarten through the 4th grade (1934-1939). His teacher was Rose Slade. Since he lived across the road from the school, he went home for lunch each day. Recess time was spent playing softball with the boys. Lawrence's family moved closer to town in 1939 and he rode the bus to White Cloud Public Schools after 4th grade. Below is a layout of the inside of the school as remembered by Lawrence.

Memories of Mary (Zacharias) Frazier

Mary Zacharias, daughter of Donald and Marie, lived on Pine Avenue when she attended Pleasant Valley School from 1951 to 1954 (Kindergarten through 3rd grade). Her teacher was Helen Waterman. Her lunch was a sandwich and cookies or Campbells soup warmed up in a pan on top of the wood boiler. Recess games included tag, Ring Around Rosie, and come on over. The students performed skits, played ball games with other schools, and had special story time when a storyteller would visit the school and use a picture board with stick on characters to tell a story.

Memories of Paul E. Thumser

Paul, son of Edwin and Irene Thumser, lived on 8th Street and attended Pleasant Valley School from Kindergarten through 6th grade (1941-1947). His teachers were Miss Clemens and Miss Waterman. He had a sandwich for lunch and played softball during recess. The softball tournament with Fry and Fulkerson Schools were memorable. The children were given the task of carrying in the wood for the wood stove. They also collected milkweed pods for the military.

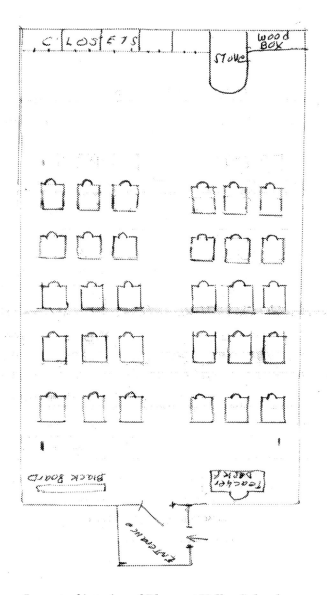

Layout of interior of Pleasant Valley School

Memories of Helen E. (Lovell) Sanders

Helen Lovell, daughter of R.D. and Kate Lovell, lived on 8th Street and attended Pleasant Valley School from 1st through 7th grade (1942-1948). Lunches included a cold sandwich with perhaps an apple and dessert (a cookie or piece of cake). Games played were Anti-I-Over, tag, dodge ball, kick the can, and softball. Special events included the Christmas programs every year and one year a traveling teacher, Gertrude Clemens, granddaughter of Samuel Clemens (Mark Twain) came and used an easel board and flannel cutouts of animals and biblical figures to tell Bible stories.

The desks had ink wells and the tops lifted up. Books could be kept in the compartment under the desk top.

Pleasant Valley School Class - Spring 1948
Front row: Jerry Bidelman, Howard Miller, Harold Miller, Gloria Eaton, Donnie
   Miller, Glen Thompson
Middle row: Tom Vickers, Jay Thompson, Norman Thompson, Sue Thompson,
   Sally Krueger, Dale Lance, Margaret Vickers, Betty Vickers
Back row: Barbara Lance, Paul Thumser, Paul Craigmyle, David Krueger,
   Conrad Thumser, Barbara Krueger, Helen Lovell, Margaret Coburn,
   teacher Helen Waterman
Missing from picture: Barbara Thumser (maried Ron Richards)

Memories of Martin J. Thompson

Martin J. Thompson, son of Norman and Alvina (Allers) Thompson Sr., lived on 8th Street and attended Pleasant Valley School for two years, 1948 and 1949 (5th and 6th grades). His teacher was Helen Waterman. The school had outhouses for restrooms, a hand pump for water, and a wood stove for heat. Games played on the playground were softball, Fox & Geese, and tag. Lunches consisted of sandwiches and fruit. Special programs recalled by Martin included 4-H, art, music, and going to the Shrine Circus.

Memories of Sue (Thompson) Totten

Sue, daughter of Frank (Bud) and Jessie Thompson, lived on E. Baseline. She attended Pleasant Valley School from 1st to 4th grade (1942-1944). Her teacher was Helen Waterman. Lunches were usually a sandwich. In cold weather, they would have a "hot lunch." The students would bring a can (home canned or store bought) of something that the teacher would mix together to make a soup which was heated over the wood stove. The students used a cloth to cover their desks and brought a bowl and spoon from home to eat with. The dishes and spoons were washed and left for use the next day. Games played were Anti I over and Mother May I. The Christmas Program was always a special event. Classmates were: Helen Lovell Sanders, Glen Thompson, Gordon Thompson, Martin Jay Thompson, Norman Thompson, Don Eaton, Margaret Vickers, Tom Vickers, Jerry Bidelman, Margaret Stuthard, Dale Lance and Barbara Lance.

Newaygo Tribune - Dec. 17, 1884 -

Everett School Report – Please publish the following school report of Dist. No. 4, Township of Everett, for the month ending Dec. 12. No. of pupils enrolled, 18. Average attendance, 16. The following names are found on the Roll of Honor: Everett Crofoot, George Cook, Estella Warren, Anna Crofoot, Cora Tripp, Sylvester Cook, Millie Cook, Henry Hornbeck, and Gertie Wilbur. Greatest number of head marks in A spelling class: Sylvester Cook; B. Class, Henry Hornbeck. Our school is progressing finely, and some improvements have been made in and about the school building during the month. Messrs. Wilbur and Tripp placed a large bell and belfry on our school house, one day last week, which we enjoyed using for two blissful days, but behold! on the third day we found it broken and ruined. Probably a flaw or the cold weather did the deed. Respectfully, Eva M. Sackett, Teacher

Memories of Patsy Lou (Thompson) Schondelmayer Long

Patsy (Pat) Thompson lived on E. Baseline, just past Poplar Avenue and Flinton Creek. Her parents were Frank (Bud) and Jessie Thompson. Pat attended Pleasant Valley School from Kindergarten through part of 4th grade and again for 5th grade and possibly 6th grade (1939-1946 or 1947). Pat's father, Frank, also attended Pleasant Valley School when he was a boy. Teachers at the school were Rose Slade, Mrs. Leah Snyder, Miss Gertrude Clemons, Mrs. Helen Waterman, Mrs. Johnson (Norma Rudert's mother).

The school had an outhouse which usually was tipped over on Halloween night. There was a hand pump outside for water and one year the water test came back marked contaminated from the Health Department. It turned out that a bird had made a nest and the water was being pumped through it. Fortunately, none of the students got sick from drinking the bad water. Lunches consisted of sandwiches made with homemade bread and a piece of dessert from previous evening's supper. A hot plate was used to heat soup one winter.

The kids played Annie (Antie) I Over, Red Rover, softball (baseball), Mother May I, various tag games and crack the whip. Kids had a slide, teeter totter and two or three swings to play on. Pat also remembers that kids would run through the entrance of the school out onto the porch step and leap over a rope held by two people.

Students took a trip to the circus one year and visited the Paris Fish Hatchery. The end of the year picnics were held at various places including the White Cloud State Park. There were also pie socials and a May Pole Dance where the girls wore white shirts with pastel color bands.

Mrs. Waterman organized a 4-H Club the last year that Pat attended school. When the boys weren't finishing their wood projects, she started a girl's wood project group to encourage competition. Both the boys and girls finished their wood projects by the finish date. The girls also finished their other projects on time too.

Other students who attended Pleasant Valley School included: Sue Thompson, Marilyn and Joyce Thompson; Dick and Helen Lovell; Daniel, Norman, Jay (possibly Glenn and Gordon too) Thompson; Conrad, Paul and Barbara Thumser; Donald and Gloria Eaton; Allen and Margaret Stuthard; Loren and Barbara Lance; Ann Tovey (and her brothers and sisters); Mumper family, Signa Cuddie; Donald Thomas; Margaret Vickers; Waybill family; Hochstetler (sp?) family.

Tripp School
School District #4

Tripp School was located in Section 28 (Section 36 at 40th and Oak?)

Teachers: Minnie Splitstone (1890), Blanch Bonner Barber (1897), Ruth Maile, Thelma Gardner, Gladys Toft

Students: Richard Toft, Douglass Bitson, Jeanette Bitson Harper, Hod and Dick Morton, Nickie Beckworth, Norma Roehrig

Sidney E. Douglass was born in 1901 in Everett Township. He attended Tripp School for eight years and carried an old dinner pail with his lunch every day. Sidney had a bit of a "devilish" streak in him and often found himself in trouble. He later graduated from Newaygo High School and Kirksville College of Osteopathy (Missouri). He was a well-known doctor and historian in White Cloud.

Tripp School

Tripp School

*Tripp School students
Circa 1890-91*

*Back row: Henry
Hornbeck, Miss Minnie
Splitstone (teacher), Mil-
lie Cook, Harry Douglass,
Elwood Hornbeck (cutoff)
    Center row: Victor Wil-
bur, Jim Cook, Gertrude
Wilbur, Nina Douglass,
Archie Cook, Bertha
Wilbur
    Front row: Nelson
Hornbeck and Grace
Angevine*

Tripp School students Spring of 1927
Front row: Norma Wilbur, Cecila Ridderikhoff, EmilyDouglass, Lila Wilbur,
Thomas Stuber, Peter Ridderikhoff, Gerald Ridderikhoff.
Back row: Floyd Wilbur, Iva Wilbur, Abby Crofoot, Susan Ridderikhoff, Jessie
Douglass, Jennie Ridderikhoff, Mr. Stuber, Mrs. Stuber, Ardella
Douglass and Doris Wilbur.
Standing in front of Emily Douglass is Norma Jean Sherwood.
Sitting on the ground in front of Tommy Stuber is the teacher Everett Douglass.

Picnic group at Tripp
School about 1920,
taken on the south side
of the school build-
ing. Left to right: Mrs.
Archie Cook, Luther
Peters, Archie Cook,
Julius Larsen, his wife,
Louise, Floyd Wilbur,
Iva, his wife, Maxwell
Crofoot, Charley Cook,
Martha Douglass and
Neva Crofoot. The three
little girls down front
belong to Floyd and Iva

Wilbur, and are Doris, Lila and Norma.
*   "For many years Luther Peters was on the school board, and as much as the teachers*
and kids pretended to dislike him, he took as much interest in the school as any board
member could, and was the only one of them ever to visit the place when it was in ses-
sion. I locked him in the woodshed once." (author unknown)

Two groups of Tripp School students

Wilcox-Union School
School District #3

Wilcox-Union School was located in Section 6.

November 16, 1900 – White Cloud Eagle

Report of District No. 3, Everett, for the month ending Oct. 26, 1900: Number days taught, 20; daily average, 15; total enrollment, 19; Roll of honor: Hazel Wright, Clyde Wright, Ettie Hocum, Laura Shelner, Tillia Shelner and Bessie Shelner. By mistake the name of Hazel Wright was omitted from the roll of honor last month. G. Annie Laing, Teacher

Newaygo Republican excerpts:

The teacher in September 1901 was Eva Sackett. There were 13 students enrolled with an average daily attendance of 11. Star scholars were Ettie Hocum, Arthur Jewett, Frank Sanford, Annie Sanford, Covell Leech, and Johnny Harris. Students listed on the Roll of Honor for the month of September were Jimmie Jones, Laura Shelner and Bessie Shelner.

September 20, 1901– "Our school closed on Sept. 19 to Honor President McKinley's funeral day, and our flag still floats at half mast in memory of his sad death."

Grant Township

Grant Township was established in 1867 by taking a six by six square mile portion of what was Croton Township. It is designated as Township 11 North, Range 12 West.

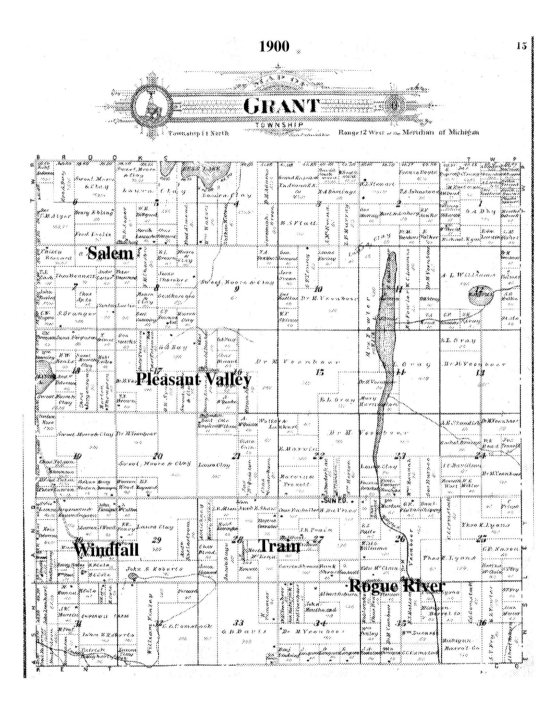

1922

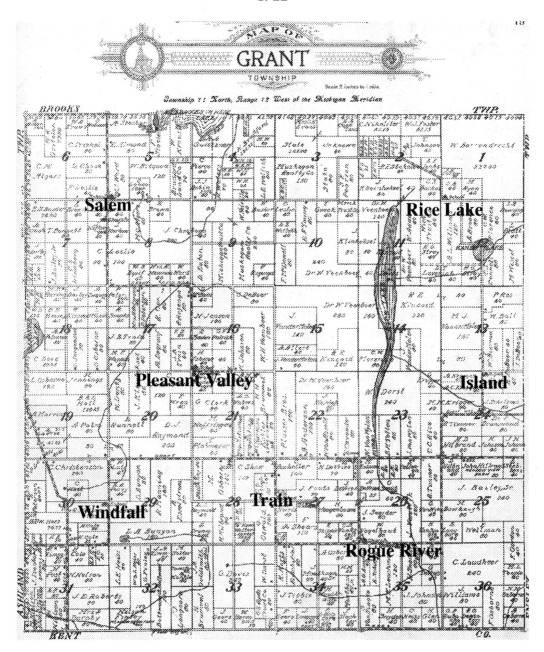

Island School
School District #6

Island School, located seven miles east of Grant at 120th and Peach Streets in Section 24, and was named for the fact that it was located on an elevation in the former Rice Lake Swamp. The original one-room frame building was built about 40 years prior to a fire that destroyed it. It had been renovated about 10 years prior to the fire which occurred about 1942. At the time of the fire, the teacher was Miss Minnie Reefman who commuted to school from her home in Fremont. The school annexed to Grant Public Schools in 1957.

Fred VanderHaag was the custodian for Island School in 1909. Newaygo County Superintendent Leon Deur gave a journal of the school's notes (1899-1932) to Greta Plaisier, granddaughter of Fred VanderHaag and she donated the journal to the NCSHG. Excerpts from the journal are as follows:

June 17, 1899 – Members of the School District #6 of Grant appointed John Beld as Moderator for three years; M.E. Hiler was elected Director for two years; and C. Kosten was elected Assessor for one year. A motion was made to procure a school site to sit as near as possible to the NE corner of SE ¼ of NW ¼ of Sec. 24, Township of Grant. A building committee was established to oversee the building of a 24'x30'schoolhouse and to buy 1 acre of land. The building committee members included John Neighbore, Martin VanDine, and Ralph Lamar.

August 19, 1899 – Rescinded the vote of 24x36 building and built a 20x30 building.

September 4, 1899 – School board approved having 7 months of school, raise $160 for teachers wages, buy 24 wood bottom chairs, purchase 10 cords of beech & maple wood to be on school grounds by Nov. 1.

September 3, 1900 – William E. Mead was elected Director for three years. Board supported holding nine months of school and to raise $250 for teacher's wages. List of books to be used: Readers for 1st through 7th grades, Elementary Arithmetics, Advances, Higher Grammar, Primary Physiology, Intermediate, Speller, Elementary Geography, McMasters History, Civil Government, Orthography, State History, and Writing Books.

March 19, 1901 – Board approved purchase of school property.

April 4, 1901 – Board closed the school to the public except for Sunday meetings.

July 8, 1901 – Board approved school for seven months.

July 11, 1904 - Board approved school for eight months.

July 10, 1905 – School to be cleaned and white washed before September. Motion made to build a barb wire fence with 7 ft. cedar posts on 3 sides of school yard

July 9, 1906 – Martin Van Duine the School Director. 9 months of school approved.

July 8, 1907 – John Beld elected Moderator for three years.

June 16, 1908 – Director resigned and Joe VanderMolen appointed to fill the vacancy

July 13, 1908 – Harry DeBoer elected treasurer; Joe VanderMolen elected Director; and M. VanTimmeran elected Moderator. Approved putting a wall and stoop on school for $50. Approved having nine months of school. Bell was to be repaired.

July 12, 1909 – H. Pastoor elected to fill vacancy. Approved nine months of school.

July 11, 1910 – Mr. Dennis elected Moderator. Approved nine months of school (same through 1915)

October 1910 – J. VanderMolen resigned and M.J. VanderMolen appointed to fill Director vacancy.

July 10, 1911 – M.J. VanderMolen elected Director and H. DeBoer was elected treasurer. Officers pay raised to $8.

July 8, 1912 – VanderMolen elected Director. Posthumus was awarded the hay on the schoolyard in consideration of 25 cents. Albert Timmer removed the sand burrs for 25 cents.

July 14, 1913 – William Bierma elected Moderator. The south and southeast side of fence moved to the school side of ditch.

July 13, 1914 – H. DeBoer elected as Director.

April 2, 1915 – A.M. Robbins hired to be the teacher for the term of nine months at $50/month.

July 12, 1915 – VanderMolen elected Director, Johannes VanWylen elected Moderator, and John Hut elected Treasurer.

May 1, 1916 – Treasurer resigned and Mrs. Jenny VanWylen appointed to fill vacancy.

July 10, 1916 – Johannes VanWylen elected Moderator and Mrs Jenny VanWylen elected Treasurer. Approved eight months of school.

July 9, 1917 – Oril Bierema elected Treasurer. 8 months of school

July 8, 1918 – J. VanderMolen elected Director. 8 months of school

July 14, 1919 – Harry DeBoer elected Director; Johannes VanWylen elected Moderator; Orie Bierema resigned as treasurer and John Scheltema elected to fill vacancy.

July 12, 1920 – William Bierema elected Treasurer. 8 months of school.

July 11, 1921 – Harry DeBoer elected Director. 9 months of school

July 10, 1922 – Johannes VanWylen elected Moderator. 8 months of school.

July 9, 1923 – William Bierema elected Treasurer. 8 months of school with 2 weeks vacation for onion topping. Motion to dig well on the south side of school.

July 14, 1924 – John Hildebrand elected Director. 9 months of school with no onion vacation.

July 13, 1925 – Gerret VanWylen elected Moderator.

July 12, 1926 – Director's salary raised to $20 and Treasurer's salary to $15. John Dykhouse elected Treasurer.

July 11, 1927 – Simon Scholten elected Director

June 11, 1928 – Gerrit VanWylen elected Moderator. Approved repairs included a new floor over the old one; a metal ceiling; a new entry with 2 cloak rooms; windows tightened.

July 12, 1929 – John Dykhouse elected Treasurer. Repairs made to the coalshed & well. New fence was raised around the school and playground equipment was purchased.

May 20, 1930 – Meeting held to find ways and means for more room as the school was getting too small. Plans were approved to remodel the school.

July 14, 1930 – Simon Scholtens was re-elected Director. Old school seats, toilets & windows were auctioned off to the highest bidder for at total of $11.20.

No notes for 1931

July 13, 1932 – K. Karp elected Moderator.

July 10, 1933 – John Dykhouse elected Treasurer

July 9, 1934 – Simon Scholtens elected Director.

July 11, 1943 – Simon Scholtens elected Director.

Former Grant resident Peter Dame offered the following information:

Island School teacher Gladys (Treiber) Shaw was born in 1903 and died 1982. Some of her students were: Jake Dykhouse, Sam Karp, Jennie Dykhouse, Jennie Karp, Stover Bol, Wilhelmina Karp, Bertha Bol, Clifford Draper, Jake Dragt, Nick Dykhouse, Martin Barends, John Dykhouse, Trinna Timmer, Eltha Draper, Dora Hilbrand, Hattie Bol, Jake Bol, Eldon Draper, and Abe Timmer.

In May 1957, Island School Board members, Gerrit VanWylen, Albert Scholtens and Charles Stray deeded the school to the Island Community Center which had just been established as a recreational center for the area. The property was sold in 1969 to Robert and Phyllis Mick and the Island Community Center non-profit organization was formally discontinued in 1972.

1938 Island School Class
Front row: Bob Veurink, Dan Veurink, Julia Ros, Howard Hiler, Johanna Hildbrand,
Jim Barry, Leona Leverich, Richard Dragt, Alice Ros, Gerald Hiler, Jeanne
Abrahams, Carl Dragt, teacher Earl Galster
Middle row: Henry Dragt, Gerald Dragt, Kathryn DeVries, Richard Hildbrand, V
ernon Porter, Bill Veurink, Al Hildbrand, Kenneth Hiler, Wilma Barends, Ila
Bos, Bob Van Wyk, Bob Barry, Alice Wert, Thelma DeVries, Jack Abrahams,
Jim Barends, Jr. Abrahams, C. Porter, Alfred Barry, ? Leverich
Back row: Opal Barry, Freida Wert, James Barry, Marjory Abrahams, Gerhard Bol,
Ruby Barry, Geneva Barends, Shirley Draper, Harry Hildbrand, Ray Hoekman

Pleasant Valley School
School District #4

Pleasant Valley School was located in Section 16 at the corner of Walnut and 120th Streets.

In 1895 Edith Stilwell taught the winter term at Pleasant Valley. Dora Brydges was the teacher at Pleasant Valley in 1937.

A 1942 photo of Pleasant Valley School

Official Membership Report
Pleasant Valley (District 4), Grant Township, Newaygo County
Teacher, Letha Anderson – School year, 1958-59

Children's Name	Grade	Parent or Guardian
Bode, Barbara	K	Herman Bode
Boone, Virginia	K	Ernest Boone
Brink, Pau	K	Peter Brink
Ferguson, Diane	K	Wesley Ferguson
Guarjardo, Gome	K	Paul Guarjardo
Guarjardo, Paul	K	Paul Guarjardo
Smith, Carl	K	Bill Smith
Santellan, Mary	K	Antiona Santellan
Leyton, Betty	K	Terry Leyton
Newton, Kirby	K	William Newton
Timmermans, Julia	K	Marvin Timmermans
Thompson, Roland	K	Ernest Thompson
Bode, Richard	1	Herman Bode
Leyton, Elex	1	Terry Leyton
Mancha, Charlie	1	Cesario Mancha
Thompson, Steven	1	Ernest Thompson
Abrahams, Gregory	2	Joe Abrahams, Jr.
Barajas, Genaro	2	Ysidaro Barajas
Ferguson, Deborah	2	Wesley Ferguson
Misner, Mary	2	Clinton Misner
Misner, Michael	2	Clinton Misner
Sanchez, Johnnie	2	Pal Guarjardo
Sawyer, Russell	2	Paul Sawyer
Smith, John	2	Bill Smith
Thompson, Ernest	2	Ernest Thompson
VanderHaag, Clare	2	Jake VanderHaag
Boone, Marvin	3	Ernest Boone
Leyton, Jerry	3	Terry Leyton
Mancha, Johnnie	3	Cesario Mancha
Nielson, Cynthia	3	Robert Nielson
Abrahams, Francis	4	Joe Abrahams, Jr.
Barajas, Estella	4	Ysidaro Barajas
Castro, San Juanita	4	Alfredo, Castro
Ferguson, Denny	4	Wesley Ferguson
Mancha, Nancy	4	Cesario Mancha
Santellan, Greg	4	Antiona Santellan
Sawyer, David	4	Paul Sawyer
VanderHaag, Albert	4	Jake VanderHaag
Leyton, Lupe	5	Terry Leyton
Mancha, Carolina	5	Cesario Mancha
Sanchez, Anna	5	Paul Guarjardo
Santellan, Theodore	5	Paul Guarjardo
Sawyer, Billy	5	Paul Sawyer
Cast, Manuel	6	Alfred Cast
Smith, Charles	6	Bill Smith

Rice Lake School
School District #7

Rice Lake was a lake marsh that had wild rice growing in it that reached heights of six to eight feet. Before the area was settled, the Indians would come every fall to harvest the rice. The lake was drained around 1916 when the Rogue River Drain was constructed so that the land could be used for growing vegetable crops (onions, celery etc.) The school was named for Rice Lake and was located at 104th and Paw Paw in Section 1.

Ruth Throop was the teacher in the fall of 1941. May Robinson was the teacher in 1948.

A 1942 photo of Rice Lake School

A 1942 photo of Rogue River School

Rogue River School
School District #5

The Rogue River School was located at 136th and Thornapple Streets in Section 35 of Grant Township. The 1900 plat map shows the school located across the street in Section 26. The origin of the name came from the school's proximity to the Rogue River.

The school closed in 1966 when the district consolidated into the Grant Public School system. The last teacher of the school was Iva Nielson.

Teachers: Ione W. Banyan (1914-15)

Jennie Sneider attended Rogue River, Longcore and Train country schools. Her favorite teacher was Eldora Clark at Rogue River School.

Memories of Margaret (Van Single) Geers

Margaret (Van Single) Geers, daughter of Sieger and Dena Van Single, attended Rogue River School from first to eighth grade. Her teacher was Mrs. Clark. The original school, built in the late 1800's or early 1900's, burned and was rebuilt. Margaret's sister started going to school in 1912. Names of classmates were Bouwkamp, Berwaltz, Anna, Jennie, Hattie and Grace Sneider, Nagelhouse, Johnson, Leseman, Osendorp, Fox, Longcore, Tibbe, Osburn and Mouthaan.

This is a photo of the first Rogue River School and students. The school was built about 1909 on the Landheer property. The school was struck by lightening and burned in 1916. It was rebuilt in 1919 across the street on the southwest corner of the Christian Leseman property.

*Rogue River
School*

Students who attended Rogue River School
No dates or identifications available for the photos on these two pages.

Rogue River School 1947
Front row: Shirley Reinink, Mary Bannink, Gayle Van Singel, Jack Mouthaan
Middle row: Marvin Hyma, Gordon Tibbe, Marilyn VerStrate, Neva Mouthaan,
Gary Van Singel, Lois Bannink, Esther Leseman
Back row: Bill Bouwkamp, Nelson VerStrate, Wayne Bannink, Ruth Leseman,
Alice Mouthaan, Lucy Mouthaan, Lloyd Bannink, Teacher Mrs. Bodell.

Rogue River School Students
Back row: Rose Lubky, three unknown boys, ? Kamphorst, unknown girl,
Clarence Bannink, unknown boy, John Slaghter, and unknown boy.
Middle row: Sara Van Singel, unknown boy and girl, Kathene Hagland, Jennie B.,
? Bouwkamp, unknown girl, boy, and girl.
Front row: Pete Van Singel, Jennie Bannink, unknown girl, the rest unknown

Teacher Grace Bodell

Grace was born on Feb. 17, 1897, the daughter of Mr. and Mrs. Delbert Eurick, and married Virgil Bodell in 1922. She taught at Rogue River School for a number of years in the 1940's. Grace died on March 16, 1988. Grace wrote the following to one of her students in January 1948:

Every cloud has a silver lining
So turn all your clouds inside out
To get this silver lining
Lovingly,
Mrs. Grace Bodell

Rogue River School Students 1937-38
Back row: Teacher Mr. Snellenberger (or Mr. Rottier?), unknown, Clifford? Longcore,
Dick Mouthaan, Clarence (Pete) Longcore, MaeRita Mouthaan, Mildred
Mouthaan, Russ (or Jim?) Osburn, Rex Robinson, Robert Mouthaan
Middle row: Gib Sneider, Marge Longcore, Hazel Osburn, Gerald Tibbe, Art Sneider,
Howard Longcore, Kathleen Geers, Laura Mouthaan, Donald Tibbe,
Bill Longcore
Front row: Tom Osburn, Lucy Mouthaan, George Landheer, Virginia Mouthaan,
Freida VanderHaag, Lawrence Bouwkamp, Helen Osburn, Ruth Leseman,
Wayne Bannink, Richard Bouwkamp

Rogue River School Students circa 1927
Front row: Arthur Hyma, Cecil Longcore, Eugene Osburn, Earl Osburn,
*   John Snyder*
2nd row: Buddy Nagleholt, Cornelia Snyder, Francis Nagleholt, Dorothy Tibbe,
*   Marjorie Mouthaan, Margaret Van Singel, Josephine Slachter, Iva Longcore,*
*   John Tibbe*
3rd row: Gertrude Snyder, Bernard Leseman, Jake Berwald, Florence Longcore,
*   Gertrude Nagleholt, Alice TenBush, Evelyn Johnson, Rollo Osburn,*
*   Edward Osburn*
Back row: Richard Johnson, Gerrit Bouwkamp, Bill Slachter, Joe Berwald,
*   Blanche DeWinter, John Nagleholt, Teacher Mrs. George (Eldora) Clark*

Rogue River School Students

Rogue River School
District No. 5
Grant Township,
Newaygo County, Michigan
1914—1915

IONE W. BRANYAN, Teacher

PUPILS

Jennie Hyma	Eunice Crispin
Benjamin Gilbert	Clarence Bannink
Sena Kamphius	Lydia Johnson
Jennie Bouwkamp	Vernie Crispin
Gerrit Slachter	Floyd Schrouder
Louis Gilbert	John Slachter
Henrietta Sneiders	Katherine Haglend
Margaret Johnson	Henry Bouwkamp
Casper Bouwkamp	Johanna Slachter
Carl Crispin	Edward Johnson
Sarah Van Singel	John Dragt
Jennie Bannink	Cornelia Hyma
Henry Dragt	Willie Van Asselt
Anna Sneiders	Frank Vellinga
James Johnson	Clarence Slachter
Joie Hilbrandt	Alice Bouwkamp
Grace Hyma	Jennie Sneiders

SCHOOL BOARD

S. Van Singel, Director   J. Van Wyke, Mod.
A. J. Bannink, Treasurer

Rogue River School Students 1945
Front row: Mary Bannink, Jack Mouthaan, Shirley Reinink, Gayle Van Singel,
*   Esther Leseman*
Middle row: Marilyn VerStrate, Gary Van Singel, Neva Mouthaan, Lois Bannink,
*   Gordon Tibbe*
Back row: Ruth Leseman, Alice Mouthaan, Marvin Hyma, Lloyd Bannink,
*   teacher Mrs. Bodell, Nelson VerStrate, Wayne Bannink, Lucy Mouthaan,*
*   Bill Bouwkamp*

Memories of Greta (VanderHaag) Knight Plaisier

Greta attended Rogue River School from 1930 to 1943. Her parents were Rynard and Anna (Snieder) VanderHaag who lived on 22 Mile Road. Greta's mother packed her a lunch which included fruit and a thermos of soup. Games played were hop scotch, leap frog and baseball. Special events were the Spelling Bees, box socials and baseball games. Greta's teachers were Mrs. Clark, Mr. Sneller and Mr. Rottier. Her parents drove her to town to attend high school.

Memories of Laurence Bouwkamp

Laurence, son of Casper and Alida Bouwkamp who lived on Oak Ave., attended Rogue River School from 1935 to 1943. His lunches consisted of sandwiches and maybe an apple or cookie. Softball was a favorite game and special events included the Christmas programs and pie socials. His teachers were Mr. Rottier, Mrs. Bodell and Mr. Snellenberger. His classmates included Longcores, Mouthaans, Osburns, Bouwkamps, Vander-Haags, Tibbes, Hymas, Snieders, Robinsons and Banninks.

Rogue River School Students 1948-1949
Front row: Kenneth Leseman, John Bouwkamp, Mary Bannink, Laura Leseman,
Beverly Reinink, Donald Van Singel, James Hyma
Middle row: Stanley Van Singel, Shirley Reinink, Lois Bannink, Neva Mouthaan,
Alice Mouthaan, Esther Leseman, Donna Larson
Back row: Gordon Tibbe, Marvin Hyma, Lloyd Bannink, Bill Bouwkamp

Memories of Gary Van Singel

Gary Van Singel, son of Ralph and Vivian Van Singel, lived on Poplar and attended Rogue River School from 1942 to 1948 (Kindergarten through 4th grade). His memories of school include lunches of homemade bread and grape jelly, playing baseball, football and swings, and the Christmas program. Mrs. Bodell and Miss Ginter were his teachers and his classmates were Lois Bannink, Wayne, Lloyd and Neva Mouthaan, Jack, Alice, Emily and Bob Landheer, and Larry, Dick, Bill and Joyce Bouwkamp.

Memories of the Landheer Family

Betty, Marilyn and Bill Landheer, children of Henry and Marie Landheer, grew up on Poplar Avenue. Betty attended Rogue River School from Kindergarten through 4th grade, Marilyn attended Kindergarten through 5th grade and Bill attended Kindergarten through 2nd grade in the early 1940's. Later, the kids went to Grant Christian School. The kids brought a sack lunch containing a sandwich and a cookie or fruit. Recess games included Innie-I-Over, pom-pom pull away, May I, and red rover. Memorable programs included the Christmas Program and the last day of school which was a fun day. Marilyn had Miss Young and Mrs. Bodell for her teachers and Mrs. Bodell was Betty and Bill's teacher. Classmates included their cousins, Bob, George, Marjorie and Ben Landheer.

Rogue River School Students 1951-1952
Front row: Kenneth Leseman, Donald Van Singel, Joyce Bouwkamp, Laura
Leseman, Keith Van Singel, Ray Logan
Middle row: James Hyma, Wayne Chase, Stanley Van Singel, Mary Bannink,
Jack Mouthaan, Gary Chase, John Bouwkamp
Back row: Teacher Miss Ginter, Esther Leseman, Donna Larson, Lois Bannink,
Neva Mouthaan, Eleanor Larson

Memories of Ruth Leseman Brown

Ruth Leseman attended Rogue River School from 1938 to 1947 (Kindergarten through 8th grade). Her parents were Chris and Elise Leseman who lived on Thornapple. Her school lunches consisted of fried egg sandwiches and cookies. Games played were red rover, Anti-I-Over, jump rope, pom pom pull away and fox & geese. The Christmas program was a special event with Evelyn Johnson playing the piano. Ruth's teachers included Miss Ginter, Pearl Wheat, Mr. Snellenburger, Mrs. Bodell, and Winifred Young. Classmates included Longcore, Tibbe, Osburn, VanderHaag, Robinson, Sneider, Leseman, Mouthaan, Bannink, Bouwkamp and Reinink.

Memories of Alice (Mouthaan) Schutter

Alice Mouthaan and her siblings, Millie, Agnes, Laura, Marjorie, Lucy, Neva, Dick and Jack, all attended Rogue River School in the late 1930's and 1940's. Alice attended from 1940 to 1948. Alice always enjoyed performing the Christmas programs for the parents. She also recalled that the mothers would make hot lunch for the students once a month.

Memories of Dick Mouthaan

   Dick Mouthaan, son of Joe and Geneva (Osburn) Mouthaan, attended Rogue River School from Kindergarten through 8th grade (1930 to 1938). The school had six big windows on the west side of the building. The large room had rows of seats for the students and a large furnace. There was also a coal bin and two cloak rooms. The students had to use outhouses for restrooms. Dick remembers having peanut butter and jelly sandwiches for lunch with a cookie once in a while. Recess games included fox & geese, tag, softball against other schools and Mayday in White Cloud. He also remembers the box socials with plays and the annual Christmas programs. His teachers were Mrs. Clark, Mr. Sneller and Mr. Rottier. After 8th grade, a group of kids took turns driving to town to attend high school. Dick's classmates included Cliff Longcore, Howard Longcore, Rex Robinson, Greta VanderHaag, Robert Mouthaan, James Osburn, Gerald Tibbe, Arthur Hyma, and George Landheer.

Memories of Jack Mouthaan

   Jack Mouthaan attended Rogue River School from Kindergarten to 8th grade (1944 to 1953). He was the son of Joe and Geneva Mouthaan and grew up on Poplar Ave. His typical lunch consisted of a peanut butter sandwich and fruit. Games played at recess time included red rover, Ante-I-Over, and ball. Special programs were the annual Christmas Program and box socials. Jack's teachers were Mrs. Bodell, Miss Ginter and Mrs. Wheat. Other families who had students at Rogue River were Tibbe, VanSingle, Hyma, Bouwkamp, Bannink, Crab, Cavender, and Chase. Jack remembers the teacher's desk was in front with the 8 rows of desks laid out with the youngest students on the teacher's left and the older students on the right. The school had a library and still used an outhouse as a restroom.

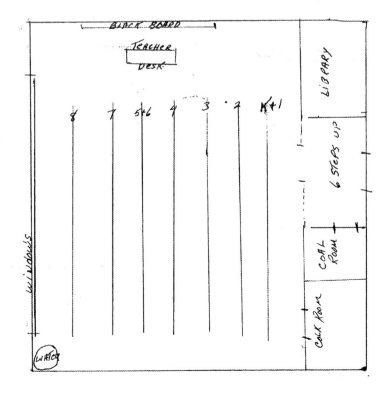

Jack Mouthaan's layout of Rogue River School

Memories of Esther (Leseman) Flynn

Esther Leseman, daughter of Bernard and Rena Leseman, grew up on 136th Street and attended Rogue River School from 1943 to 1952. A typical lunch was sandwiches and fruit, but once a month the students' mothers brought in hot food. Games played at recess included red rover, Anni-I-Over, and jump rope. In the winter, the kids also slid down Leseman hill on tin refrigerator doors and ice skated on frozen ponds in the Landheer pasture. Special programs were the Christmas plays, Valentine's Day party and the end of the year school picnic. Esther's teachers were Miss Winfred Young, Mrs. Grace Bodell, Miss T. Ginter, and Pearl Wheat. After finishing 8th grade, Esther rode the bus (driven by Sheriff Bill Brown) to high school. Students that Esther remembers attending Rogue River School included Wayne, Lloyd, Lois and Mary Bannink, Lucy, Alice, Neva and Jack Mouthaan, Ruth Leseman, Pearl and Joyce Crabb, Gary and Wayne Chase, Shirley Reinink, Gordon Tibbe, Marvin Hyma, Donna and Eleanor Larson, Stanley, Donald and Keith Van Singel, Raymond, Nancy and Lee Logan, Michael and Cynthia Hiler, George, Ben and Bob Landheer, Marilyn, Betty and Bill Landheer, Lawrence, Betty, Richard, John, Bill, Joyce and Nancy Bouwkamp.

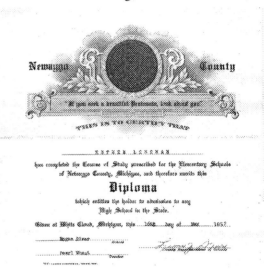

Esther Leseman's 8th grade diploma

Memories of Joyce (Bouwkamp) Cammenga

Joyce Bouwkamp attended Rogue River School from 1949 to 1958. Her parents were Casper and Alida (Van Galen) Bouwkamp. Her father also attended Rogue River School circa 1909. As an adult he bought his father's farm on Oak Street and sent his four sons to Rogue River School. The family moved to 128th Street just prior to Joyce starting school. She believes that because two of her brothers were still attending Rogue River School, her father paid tuition so that all the Bouwkamp children (Laurence, Richard, William, John, Nancy & Joyce) could go there. Joyce's parents drove them to school every day because they lived two and one half miles away. Along the way, they would pick up other kids heading to school. The kids usually walked home (at least part of the way) after school. Joyce recalls that there was one old man in the neighborhood who drove a team of huge black horses and if they saw him coming on the road, they moved as close to the ditch as they could get because they were frightened of the horses.

Teachers at Rogue River School included Eldora C. Clark (about 1929) Mrs. Bergman, Mr. Rottier, Mr. Orville Snellenberger, Mrs. Grace Bodell, Miss Young, Terveer Ginter (1948-1951), Pearl Wheat (1951-1953), Rachel Crispin (1953-1955), Irene Slachter (1955-1958), Shirley Renney and Ivah Nielsen. Joyce's teachers were Terveer Ginter,

Pearl Wheat, Rachel Crispin, Irene Slachter and Mrs. Potts (a substitute at the time Joyce graduated). Miss Ginter, who was from Indiana and didn't have a car, boarded at either the Henry Van Singel or Al Shears residence while she was teaching.

The school was located on the north side of 136th at the corner of Thornapple. In 1916 after lightning struck the school and burned it down, the school was rebuilt across the street on the southwest corner. Outhouses were used the first couple of years that Joyce went to school, then indoor restrooms were installed.

Joyce's lunches consisted of a sandwich, fruit, a cookie or cake. She also had hot chocolate which she brought in a thermos. According to news clippings that Joyce has, the school was the smallest school (possibly in the state) to have a hot lunch program in 1952. She remembers that recess was always fun. The kids played hide and seek, softball, volleyball, fox and geese, tag, and a game the kids called 6 and 4. Because it was a small school, everyone was needed for games -- even the smallest kids were included.

Joyce remembers the annual Christmas program when the "big boys" would get the boards out of the attic and fit them together just right to form the stage. A heavy wire was stretched in front of it to hang the "curtain" on. A big Christmas tree was put up in the front corner and the kids drew names to see who they would buy a gift for. Songs were practiced and play parts were given out and memorized. Costumes were put together and they always had the nativity acted out. The school house was always packed with family for the program and everyone would try to guess who would play Santa at the end of the program resulting in lots of excitement. Evelyn Johnson, who lived close by, would come and play the piano for the singing. The kids practiced hard and when the night of the program came they peeked from behind the curtain at the audience. The teacher stood behind the curtain to prompt the kids if stage fright caused them to forget their lines. The day after the program, the kids went to school and took down the stage, the tree, and all the Christmas decorations. The school was cleaned and made ready for work after a well deserved Christmas vacation.

Another special day was the school picnic held on the final day of school. In the morning, the students put away their books and cleaned out their desks. At noon, the mothers brought a wonderful potluck dinner. After lunch, the school board president came with a big container of ice cream packed in dry ice. The afternoon was filled with games, fun and all the ice cream they could eat. The mothers would have a good visit before packing up the kids and the picnic stuff and then head for home for summer vacation. On Halloween, the kids had a costume contest and played games and on Valentine's Day they exchanged valentine cards and had a party.

In 1946, a Christian school was started in the neighborhood which took many kids out of the Rogue River School.

Students Joyce remembers attending Rogue River School include Delores, David, Steve, Rolland, and Marilyn Tibbe, Donna and Eleanor Larsen (they lived with Cavenders), Neva and Jack Mouthaan, Esther, Kenneth (Bob) and Laura Jean Leseman, Lois, Mary and Elaine Bannink, Gary and Wayne Chase, Stan, Don, Keith, Linda, and Russell Van Singel, Jim and Bruce Hyma, John, Joyce and Nancy Bouwkamp, Raymond, Nancy and Lee Logan, Shirley and Beverly Reinink, Otis Shears, Howard and Rosella Hall, Jerry Puite, and the Hallie family attended for one year.

Rogue River School Students 1959
Front row: Gordon Puite, Lee Logan, Bruce Hyma, Steve Tibbe, Jerry Puite,
    George Dewey
Back row: Teacher Miss Renney, Russell Van Singel, David Tibbe, Nancy Logan,
    Elaine Bannink, Nancy Bouwkamp, Rozella Hall, Howard Hall, Delores
    Tibbe, Linda Dewey, Linda Van Singel

Memories of Lois (Bannink) Schuitema
    Lois, daughter of Henry and Henrietta Bannink, attended Rogue River School from Kindergarten through 8th grade (1943 to 1950). Her family lived on Poplar. Lois remembers going outside each morning to pump water for drinking and washing hands. In back of the school room was a water fountain and a wash basin. Each desk had an ink well. and the rows of desks faced the teacher with the younger students on one side and the older students on the other. The school had a library, a cloak room for the boys and another for the girls as well as a furnace room and a storage room. There was a flag pole outside and the flag was put up each morning and taken down at the end of the day. School lunches consisted of a sandwich, a sweet, and fruit (when available). Recess games played were Inny-I-Over, and red rover, red rover. Special programs held were Valentines Day, Christmas Program, picnics and the last day of school potluck. Her teachers were Mrs. Bodell and Miss Terveer Ginter. After 8th grade, Lois rode a bus an hour to an hour and a half to attend high school. Classmates included Jack, Neva, Alice, and Lucy Mouthaan, Lois, Lloyd, Mary and Elaine Bannink, Bouwkamps, Van Singels, Larsons, Lesemans, Landheers, and Shirley Reinink.

Memories of Elaine (Bannink) Moore

Elaine was a student at Rogue River School from 1953 to 1961. Her parents were Henry and Henrietta Bannink who lived on Poplar. By the 1950's the school had indoor plumbing and two bathrooms as well as a kitchen. Elaine remembers that the first few years that she attended school, there was a cook that came and made hot lunches. Mothers of the students gathered together each summer and fall to can vegetables and fruit for the winter. The Christmas program was always a big event for the kids. Elaine remembers that the students would build a stage with curtains on the sides and front and would practice their lines for a couple of weeks prior to the program. Elaine's teachers were Mrs. Wheat, Mrs. Slaghter, Miss Renney and Mrs. Bergman. Her classmates included John, Nancy and Joyce Bouwkamp, Ray, Nancy, and Lee Logan, Laura and Bob Leseman, Delores, Dave, Marilyn, Barb, and Steve Tibbe, Keith, Russ, and Linda Van Singel, Gerald and Jerry Puite, Jim, Bruce and Don Hyma, and Gary and Wayne Chase. After 8th grade, Elaine rode the bus to attend Grant High School.

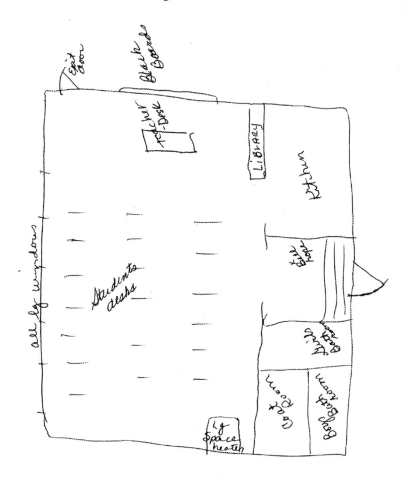

Elaine Bannink Moore's layout of Rogue River School which
shows the addition of a kitchen and indoor restrooms.

Rogue River School Reunion

(Author Unknown)

(Courtesy of Rogue River School Reunion Committee)

We pause a moment at the door
While eager hearts race on ahead.
We long to follow on swift feet,
But walk with dignity instead.

We meet again as old friends do,
At first constrained by passing years;
But classmates' faces soon take form,
And hand clasps hand amid brief tears.
The slim, young girls are matrons now;
The boys are men grown older, gray.
But each has lived a rich, full life
And gained in stature in his way.

Some paths have crossed to meet again;
Some stars have dimmed and burn no more.
On some, success has left its mark,
And some show sorrows that they bore.

A stealthy glance at printed named
Brings youthful image fresh to mind;
A metamorphosis takes place
That glows upon a face that's lined.

And suddenly the years recede;
The time between has ceased to be;
And we are classmates once again,
The carefree friends we used to be.

Rogue River School Reunions 2005 (above) and 2006 (below)

*Two views of
Salem School*

Salem School
School District #3

Salem School was located at 104th and Willow Streets in Section 5. The school closed in 1962 and the building is now a church (2011). It may have had the nickname of Ranglebird School. The school had a caretaker in the late 1950's, early 1960s named Mr. Frickell.

Teachers: Mrs. Janet Abfalter (1936-1937); Ella Bender (1941); Mrs. Tanis; Mr. Weaver; Mrs. Rachel Crispin, Velma Matson (1948).

Memories of Mary Lockery (Buckner)

Mary (Buckner) Lockery, daughter of Erma and Winfield Buckner, grew up on 104th Street in Grant. She attended Salem (Rangleburg) School for 6th and 7th grades and her teacher was Mrs. Ella Bender. A typical lunch consisted of sandwich, apple, piece of cheese, boiled egg and milk. Games played on the playground were jump rope, tag and marbles. Special programs were Christmas plays and fire drills (outside fire escape). Inside bathrooms (chemical?). Classmates included Joann Pressler, Irene Frickle, Barbara Lake, Donna Sharp, Nathan and Lee Baker, Irene Jones, Gloria Lake, Clifford Sharp, Wayne Robinson, Joy Newton, Robert Viayl, Judy Gibson, and Charles Frickle.

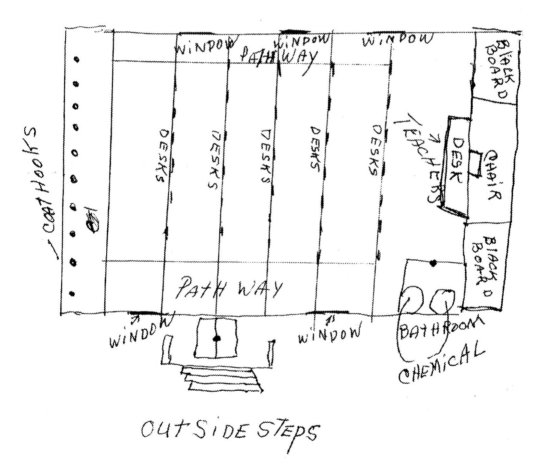

Mary (Buckner) Lockery drew this layout of what she
remembers of the inside of Salem School.

Train School

Train School
School District #1

The Train School was built in 1866 or 1869 and was the first rural school built in Grant Township. It was named after the Train family and was located at 132nd and Spruce Streets in Section 27.

The first schoolhouse was a 16x24 foot log building that was built on J.H. Mannings land. The desks and seats were made of unplaned boards and placed around the room next to the wall. A new, frame schoolhouse replaced the log building about 1876 or 1878 and was located on Train family land about a half a mile south of the original school. This school burned in 1901 or 1910 and was replaced by a cement building.

Four generations of the Train family attended Train School - John B. Train, a pioneer settler; John's daughter, Leona McQuistian; Leona's son, Lawrence Hannigan Train; and Lawrence's daughter Barbara (married Harley Stroven).

In the early years, the school year was only two to three months at at time. The teacher received up to $2 per week pay with free board, staying with area host families.

Among the first students to attend Train School were John Train, Lettie, Henry and Lyman Shaw, Anna and Herman Marvin and Frank and Nettie Glover.

Train School Teachers: Rose North, Marian Allen, Phila Hues, Florence DeWitt, Dora McNitt, Libby Gibson, Henry Race, Zina Madison, Minnie Pintler, Nancy Alvord, Johnny Battles, Ernest Dowd, Nettie Phelps, Will Barnum, Bennie Faunce, Earl Evans, Walter Woolford, Arthur Rich, Maggie Gorman, Rosie Cronks, Carrie Judd, Lizzie Rupp, and Millie (Hall) Pollard, Mrs. Dora Maskey (1937), Anna Rossiter (1940), Halla Lovell (1941), Gladys Brown (1948).

Newaygo Republican excerpts:

Report of Grant Township, School District 1, month ending May 11, 1895 – 43 pupils enrolled. Pupils neither absent or tardy: Erma Stanton, Susie Brackett, Pearl Brackett, Mabel Baker, Mary Cavender, Blanche Bacheller, Vene Shears. Frances Peacock, Teacher.

School District 1, Grant Township, report for month ending June 7, 1895. 43 pupils enrolled. Pupils not absent: Inez Cavender, Mary Cavender, Libbie Bacheller, Mac Brackett, Pearl Brackett, Blance Bacheller, Leo Bacheller, Vene Shears. Frances Peacock, Teacher.

School District 1 in Grant Township, report for term ending July 4, 1895. 44 pupils enrolled. Not absent: Blanche Bacheller, mary Cavender, Pearl Brackett. Frances Peacock, Teacher.

An early Train School Class

Memories of Edward Ausema

Edward Ausema attended Train School from 1943 to 1952 (Kindergarten through 7th grade). He lived near Spruce and 136th Street with his parents John and Gertrude Ausema. His school lunch consisted of a sandwich and sometimes an apple. At recess the kids played red rover, drop the handkerchief, softball and eenie eye over.

Special events were the Christmas program and the end of the year picnic. Edward's teachers were Violet Ordish and Gladys Brown. The school had an "indoor outhouse". After country school he took the bus to town to attend school. His classmates were Loretta, George, Marjorie, Josephine, Gordon and Eugene Atwood, Billy and Carol Jean Bolthouse, June Ann Brummel, Nelson, Lois and Shirley Zoet, Carol Kay and Wayne Kruithof, Ron Geers, Nancy Emorey, Marion and Gerald Hilbrand, Delores Scholtens, Gary and Gayle Van Singel, Helen and Cornelius Ausema.

Edward Ausema's certificates promoting him to the 5th and 7th grade.

RATINGS

A—Does very good work   D—Below average
B—Does well, above average   E—Failure
C—Does as well as average   I—Incomplete

SUBJECTS	1ST SEMESTER					2ND SEMESTER				
	1	2	3	Exam	Sem. Av.	1	2	3	Exam	Sem. Av.
Arithmetic	B	B	B+	4.4	B	B	B	B	5.1	B
Arts	A	A	A		A	A	A	A-		A
English	B	B	B	3.7	B	B+	B+	B	5.4	B
History				3.8					5.0	
Health	A	A			A	A	A	A		A
Penmanship	A	A	A		A	A	A	A		A
Literature Reading	B	B	B	3.7 / 3.7	B	B	B	A-	4.5 / 4.5	B+
Spelling	B+	B+	A	4.6	B+	B+	A-	A	4.0	A
Geography	B	B+	B+	5.0	B+	B+	B+	B-	5.4	B
Science				4.4					4.5	
Civics and Current Events										
Music										
Average				4.1					4.8	
Days Absent	2½	0	1			1½	0	0		
Times Tardy	0	0	0			0	0	0		

CHARACTER, EDUCATION AND CITIZENSHIP

The following good habits and attitudes are desirable for good school citizenship. The teacher has marked only those which are particularly noticeable.

	PERIOD					
	1	2	3	4	5	6
Is prompt and punctual	✓	✓	✓	✓	✓	
Uses time to good advantage	✓	✓	✓		✓	
Is neat of self, work and desk	✓	✓	✓	✓	✓	
Has good sitting, standing and walking position	✓	✓	✓			
Is careful of own and school property	✓	✓	✓	✓	✓	
Is courteous and considerate of others	✓	✓		✓	✓	
Follows directions	✓	✓	✓	✓	✓	
Is obedient and respects authority	✓	✓		✓	✓	
Does not give up easily	✓	✓	✓	✓	✓	
Accepts criticism and tries to improve	✓	✓	✓	✓	✓	

Dear Parent:

If your child is weak in some habits or attitudes perhaps you can help him to improve himself in these.

Some Desirable Habits and Attitudes

Following are some of the habits most essential to the wholesome development of the child which the school and the home should try to develop.

Health Habits:

Sits, stands, and walks in healthful posture.
Tries to improve his health.
Protects health of others.
Sleeps ten hours each night in a well ventilated room.
Eats proper food.
Bathes often.
Cleans teeth daily.

Work Habits:

Is prompt and ready to work.
Makes good use of time.
Does not easily give up.
Is thorough and careful in his work.
Follows directions.
Works and plays willingly with others.
Helps in class planning, discussions and work.

Personal Habits:

Uses good judgment.
Accepts criticism in good spirit and tries to improve.
Has self confidence.
Takes pride in personal appearance.

Social Habits:

Is considerate of others.
Is careful of own and school property.
Is obedient and respects leadership.
Is reliable and assumes responsibility.

Reed City—The Copper Press—White Cloud

NEWAYGO COUNTY PUBLIC SCHOOLS
Report of Pupil's Progress

Name *Edward Ausema*

Grade *4*   Promoted to grade *5*

School *Train*

School Year 19*47* to 19*48*

Teacher *Violet Ordish*

* Parent's Signature

1. *J. Ausema*
2. *J. Ausema*
3. *J. Ausema*
4. *J. Ausema*
5. *J. Ausema*
6. ....

*Note: Your signature means only that you have seen the card.

TO PARENTS: It is the purpose of our schools to have your child enjoy his education, and to have him develop and grow steadily, not only in mind, but in character as well. We must remember that children need to learn, not only subject matter, but also how to live together and become good citizens.

Providing a child with an education is a community undertaking. The home must share with the school the responsibility for developing desirable traits of character and proper attitudes toward life. Your cooperation will be appreciated by the teachers and they will be glad to discuss with you concerning your child's progress.

LEON J. DEUR,
County School Commissioner

Edward Ausema's 4th grade report card

1946 Train School Class
Back row: Bert Skipper, Donna Van Wylen, Carol DeVries, Clara Osborn,
*   Jerlane Vanderwaude, Marian Hilderbrand, Laurita Atwood,*
*   Josephine Atwood, Jerry Plaisier*
Middle row: Nelson Zoet, Harold Plaisier, Gordon Pluhler, Barbara Plaisier,
*   Berdine Skipper, Mary Ann Pluhler, Cornelius Ausema, George Atwood*
Front row: Edward Ausema, Gerald Hilderbrand, Marjorie Atwood, unknown,
*   Ronald Geers, Lois Zoet, unknown, Ralph Shears, Gordon Atwood,*
*   unknown*

Memories of George Atwood Jr.

George Atwood Jr., son of George E. and Josephine Atwood, lived on Walnut Avenue and attended Train School from 1939 to 1947 (Kindergarten through 7th grade). His typical lunch was a sandwich, fruit and hot chocolate. Games played at recess were tag, tackelina and softball. The Christmas program was the special event of the year with all the students participating. George's teachers were Miss Anna Rossiter and Mrs. Ordish. The school had an indoor cesspool type bathroom (no flush). George Atwood and Nelson Zoet were responsible for starting the fire in the school in the winter time. After the 7th grade, he took the bus to town to attend school. Students of the school included Raymond, Bernetta, Laurita, George and Marjorie Atwood, Josephine and Gordon Atwood, William Atwood Jr., Clara and Harold Osborn, Douglas Mouthaan, Herbert VanWylen, Ronald, Lois, and Marilyn Geers, Carol Kruithoff, Nelson, Lois, and Shirley Zoet, Helen and Cornelius Ausema, Edward Ausema, Carol and Billy Botlhouse, Nancy Emorey, Lillian Hoogenboon, Gertrude Hoogenboon, Jerlane and Al Vanderwoude, Lawrene Scott, ? Badger, Josephine, Gerald and Marian Hilbrandt, Gloria, Larry and Manuel Muiz, Harold, Barbara, Jerry, Henrietta, and Florence Plaisier, Gordon and Marian Peuler, and Ralph Shears.

These are memories as best remembered by Josephine, Gordon and Eugene Atwood, children of Lawrence and Margaret Atwood:

Train school sat on a high hill between 128th Street and 136th Street. The school was on Spruce Avenue, Grant Township, Newaygo County. The building was a solid cement block school. The south side of the building was lined with windows. This side of the school faced to the south and this is where the playground area was. The school had a small basement room for the coal furnace. The furnace started out using lamp coal and later a Stoker Furnace was installed. The basement had a small room for the furnace and the rest of the basement was just a crawl space. The school was mainly a one room classroom school with two entry doors. This front area stretched across the width of the front of the school. As you came in one door there was the bell rope and a small area for books we could read. This was also where we would hang coats and leave our boots. There was also a very small back room for teaching activities. This area was at the far end opposite the cloak area with the large one room classroom in the middle. In this very small room, at times, a store was set up for students to sell items to other students, such as candy, pencils, and treats. I'm sure this was to teach math skills and how to count change and add items up that were being bought. This area also had the boys and girls bathrooms. These bathrooms were "non-flushing" toilets. The stairs to go to the furnace room was also back there. Gordon said the children all had small chores to do. The older boys put the coal in the furnace and different children were called on to ring the bell for school to start.

Josephine Atwood attended the school from 1937 through 1946. Her teachers were Anna Rossiter, Hala Lovell and Violet Ordish. (In later years, Mrs. Ordish became the Grant Librarian for many years.)

Train School 8th Graders in 1946 (left to right): Bert Skipper, Donna Van Wylen, Jerlane Vanderwaude, Laurita Atwood, Josephine Atwood, Barbara Plaisier

Gordon Atwood attended the school from 1944 to 1952 and his teachers were Violet Ordish and Gladys Brown.

Eugene Atwood attended the school from 1947 to 1955 and his teachers were Violet Ordish, Gladys Brown and Leetha Anderson.

Josephine recalls the fun times in the winter. Some of the children would take sleds to the hill not far from the school during the noon lunch time. The teacher would ring the bell three times about fifteen minutes before time for classes to start so the children had time to get back. Other times the bell was rung just one time.

We would go to different country schools to play softball. The teacher would get as many children as possible into her car and the rest of the children would ride on the running boards or fenders of the car.

There are great memories of the Christmas programs and setting up the stage and the curtains for the Christmas program. The boys usually did this. We had a beautiful Christmas tree that was usually donated to the school. We all got to help decorate the classroom with red and green chains that everyone helped to make and also taking red and green crape paper and twisting it in spirals to hang from the ceiling to each corner of the room. Everyone had a part in the Christmas program. There was singing, plays and poems to recite and many days of practice to get ready for the program. When it was finally time for the Christmas program and the school was filled with parents and relatives and not even standing room was left. When the program was over it was time for Santa. He would come running in and ringing his bells with a "HO,HO,HO," and then the gifts would be handed out for our name exchanges. In the later years, Gordon learned that Peter Osborn had been the Santa and after him, Simon Kruitoff was the Santa.

Train School students
June Ann Brummel,
Kenneth Van Asselt,
Edward Ausema,
Lois Zoet

Train School 7th Graders in 1945 (left to right): Barbara Plaisier, Josephine Atwood, Jerlane Vanderwaude, Laurita Atwood, Donna Van Wylen, Bert Skipper

Train School teacher Mrs. Violet Ordish

Train School 1943-44 Students

Train School Students Fall 1947
Back row: Teacher Mrs. Violet Ordish (husband Clyde), Marjorie Atwood, Sue Bodell,
William Bolthouse, Edward Ausema, Cornelius Ausema, Ronald Geers
Front row: Gordon Atwood, Lois Zoet, Shirley Zoet, Carol Jean Bolthouse,
Carol Kay Kruithoff, Helen Ausema, Flourencia (last name unknown,
migrant worker family), Eugene Atwood

*Train School
1946-1947 Class
Back row: Nelson
Zoet, George Atwood,
teacher Mrs. Violet
Ordish
Middle row: Mar-
jorie Atwood, Edward
Ausema, Gordon
Atwood, Cornelius
Ausema, Billy Bol-
thouse, Ronald Geers
Front row: Carol
Kay Kruithoff, Lois
Zoet, Shirley Zoet,
Helen Ausema, Carol
Jean Bolthouse,
Nancy Lee Emmorey*

Train School Students 1947
Back row: Cornelius Ausema, Martha Bolle, George Atwood, Nelson Zoet
*2nd row: Gordon Atwood, Billy Bolthouse, Ronald Geers, Edward Ausema, Lois Zoet,
Joe Bolle, Marjorie Atwood*
*Front row: Helen Ausema, Shirley Zoet, Carol Kruithoff, Donna ?, Carol J. Bolthouse,
Lynn ?, Nancy Emmorey*

Memories of Carol (Kruithoff) George

Carol Kay (Kruithoff) George lived on 132nd Street, a dead-end road off of Spruce. Her parents were Simon and Jeanette Kruithoff. Carol attended Train School from Kindergarten through the 7th grade (1946-1954). She remembers eating sandwiches and cookies for lunch and playing baseball and hide and go seek during recess. She especially remembers teacher Mrs. Anderson teaching the girls sewing for 4-H meetings. Besides Mrs. Leatha Anderson, other teachers that taught at Train School were Gladys Brown and Violet Oridsh. The school did have indoor plumbing. Carol continued her education by walking a quarter mile to catch the bus to travel to Grant Public Schools for high school. Carol's parents farmed 100 acres and owned the Train property where the school house once was.

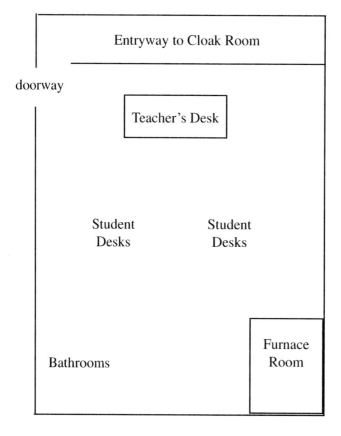

The layout of Train School

An early Train School Class

Train School teacher
Leatha Anderson
1954-1955

Windfall School
School District #2

Windfall School was built in 1886 and was located in Section 30 at 132nd and Willow. May Brower was the teacher there for several years including the years 1937-1941. Dorothy Ames was the teacher in 1948.

A 1942 photo of Windfall School (above) and a photo taken in the 1980s (below)

Etta Ackland and a Litany of One
By Jackie Deater
Times-Indicator - July 7, 1982

When Etta Ackland graduated from school, she was like most teenagers. She wasn't sure what she wanted to do, but was sure she wanted to do something.

Not inclined toward any young man at the time, marriage wasn't an option. But she did love children. She had grown up with seven siblings, and had experienced a happy childhood, so she decided to spread some of that joy. She decided to go into teaching.

At age 18 she graduated from Newaygo County Normal School – a teacher's college operating in the Fremont High School building. She began teaching the following fall in Windfall School in Grant.

For $55 a month, she taught there for a year, living in Branyon's Boarding House during the week and hitching a ride home to Newaygo by train on weekends. Sometimes her parents would drive her back to Grant in their new car which had curtains around the windows, but driving on Sundays was frowned upon.

After that initial year of teaching, she taught in several other one-room schoolhouses, including Garfield Center (now the township hall); Butler School in Fremont; Kimball Lake School; and Newaygo School. Her teaching career spanned 41 years, and all were spent in one-room schoolhouses except the last 18, when she was a Newaygo Junior High School teacher and administrator.

As part of the teacher's contract back in the early 1900's, Ackland was required to continually take teaching courses to renew her three year teaching certificate. She said teachers would do this through correspondence courses, summer school, and with the help of teachers from Western Michigan University who would travel north to teach the local instructors.

But it wasn't until she was 56-years-old that she received her formal degree from WMU.

"I never spent a full year in college and I taught 41 years," she chuckled.

After teaching seven years in three different schools, she found that young man to fall in love with. While a teacher in Newaygo the first time around, she met Oscar Anderson, a "neighborhood boy," and they married. Soon after, they had a son, Richard, and Ackland gave up teaching for three years.

Her next assignment was Kimball Lake School, which has since burned down, and while there, she had a daughter, Marilyn. Born Christmas Day, four years after Richard was born, Ackland remembers Marilyn's birth vividly. "No one knew I was pregnant. I worked the Friday before Christmas and she was born on Sunday."

During the Depression, Ackland worked at Butler School, then transferred to Newaygo Junior High School in 1944.

She and Oscar bought the farm she still lives on at 1351 68th Street in 1926. After doing chores one night in 1941, Oscar lay down and died, leaving her with a second grader and a sixth grader. But she kept working for 21 more years.

She retired from Newaygo Junior High School in 1962 and in 1964 married Fred Ackland, a lifelong friend and owner of Ackland Fruit Orchards.

She moved to the orchards when she married Fred, but retained her home and rented it out, sensing that someday she might want to return. After Fred's death in 1978, she sold the orchards, and returned to her farm, which is adjoined by a house owned by her daughter Marilyn Melvin, husband Donald and their daughter Jackie.

Ackland said a lot has changed since she began teaching. Teachers were given a course of study they had to follow back then which stressed reading, writing, arithmetic and poetry. Now they have more choices.

And kids have changed, too. "Communication and transportation has made so much change in children's lives that there can't help but be a change," she remarked.

But she doesn't see that as necessarily bad. "There's always been good and bad kids."

At age 82, Ackland now spends her time at Senior Citizens activities, church functions, Ladies' Aide Society, and keeping her lovely house immaculate.

"I've had a good life," she says.

Country School
By William Maloney

Many great men
Have begun their journey to fame,
In a one-room schoolhouse
On a dusty country lane.

Where desks of scarred wood,
Engraved through the years,
Have seated future presidents
And a hundred other careers.

Where they have stood and taught,
Whose own castles high
Have never known the sunlight
Of a golden sunlit sky.

Who have turned their minds instead
To teaching innocent youth
The knowledge they possess,
That children better know the truth.

Thus children have learned
That greatness is a flame,
And knowledge the fuel
That kindles the spark of fame.

And no matter how small the beginning,
A country school it might well be,
Where greatness will rise up
To write a page in history.

Unknown Schools & Students

 The following pages contain photos of schools and students which do not have identifications. If anyone can identify the school name or any of the students, the Newaygo County Society of History and Genealogy would greatly appreciate the information. Information may be sent by mail to PO Box 68, White Cloud, MI 49349 or by email at newaygocohistory@yahoo.com.

1930-31 Class